Point of Departure

Other books in the series are:

ENCOUNTERS Stage 1
ENCOUNTERS Stage 2
ENCOUNTERS Stage 3
ENCOUNTERS Stage 4
TWENTIETH CENTURY ENCOUNTERS—BRITISH AUTHORS
INTERNATIONAL ENCOUNTERS—THE TWENTIETH CENTURY
EARLY ENCOUNTERS

ENCOUNTERS STAGE 5

Point of Departure

John Watts

PRINCIPAL, COUNTESTHORPE COLLEGE:
FORMERLY LECTURER IN THE ENGLISH DEPARTMENT
AT THE UNIVERSITY OF LONDON INSTITUTE OF EDUCATION.

LONGMAN

LONGMAN GROUP LIMITED
London
*Associated companies, branches and representatives
throughout the world*

© *John Watts* 1965

*All rights reserved. No part of this publication may be
reproduced, stored in a retrieval system or transmitted in
any form or by any means—electronic, mechanical,
photocopying, recording or otherwise—without the prior
permission of the copyright owner.*

First published 1965
Tenth impression 1978

ISBN 0 582 21651 6

*Printed in Hong Kong by
Yu Luen Offset Printing Factory Ltd*

*To my colleagues at
Crown Woods School, Eltham*

Introduction

This is a book for school-leavers—pupils in their last year at school, students in their first year out of school. It aims to relate the themes of social studies with leisure reading, to show how the world we live and work in is illuminated by literature.

Literature should not be formidable, meaning, as it does, what people have written down. It is the books that people enjoy reading, in which they find an extension to and reflection of their own lives. In *Point of Departure* it is represented by some thirty books, mostly written by living authors, mostly available in paperback editions. Only books that are likely to be read right through have been chosen, and so they could well be in the school library, or as a set on the classroom shelf.

The twelve themes which form the framework of this book could be the basis of a social studies course. They start from the known and local, Home and About, moving out in widening circles through the activities of Work and Leisure, to the broader subjects of the World Community.

It will be a great advantage if the pupils using *Point of Departure* are also following a social studies course based on a similar outline: the possibilities for correlation are many. But the volume can be used independently, so long as it is understood that the reading and follow-up work in each chapter cannot possibly exhaust the subject. It is intended only to show that the subjects of concern to the young person, which can so often remain impersonal, unrelated to anything already being experienced, can touch the imagination and take on life when seen through the writing of a novelist, poet, playwright or biographer. Too often our presentation of subjects at school implies an order, a tidiness, even a finality which is not true to the world of experience. In experience the affairs of this life are more usually untidy, inconclusive and, mercifully, unpredictable. Only the artist can make sense out of this confusion without falsifying it, and *Point of Departure* is intended to help the teacher introduce readers to this clarifying experience of literature.

Each chapter follows a more or less uniform pattern. It incorporates two or three extracts, each introduced by brief questions that relate the abstract theme to particulars well within the pupil's experience.

INTRODUCTION

These questions are best taken orally, but they should not hold up an early start on reading the extract. (They could sometimes be posed in advance, say at the end of the lesson before that in which the extract is to be read, and they could sometimes be set as homework.)

The extracts are of a length to make them worth reading for their own sakes; some of them are complete chapters from novels, one is a complete short story. Taken alone with the notes on books and authors at the end of the volume, they would form a useful anthology. The teacher may wish to read some of the extracts in class (certainly the play scenes and the poem need this treatment), or they may be set for private or home reading, so that class time can be devoted to the follow-up work.

The follow-up work on each extract falls into three parts. The 'Questions' seek to draw attention to essential points in the extract. They are a test of comprehension, but also of imagination and discrimination. They can be used by the teacher to point out the thread of the narrative or argument. Although for many of these questions there is a correct answer, they cannot be answered (or corrected) mechanically: most of them are worded so as to encourage individual forms of answer. There is scope for opinion, but they are essentially questions on the text.

In the second section, 'Implications', questions are asked that return the readers to the theme, taking up and sometimes repeating the introductory questions. These questions are open-ended, having no right or wrong answers. They call instead for personal recollections, opinions, comments on logical and social questions. They start with questions posed by reading the extract and thus make an oblique approach to the pupils personally, and give less chance for mere prejudices to prompt the answers.

It is hoped that this section will be dealt with in open discussion. Very often the value of these questions lies in the hares that they will start. They were framed in the belief that controlled group discussion is one of the most fruitful learning situations and they have been put to the test in the classroom. Most teachers and classes will modify and supplement the questions in their own way, making them the basis of their own discussion. Written answers may be given to these questions, although this will depend on the degree of literacy of the pupils. They are often difficult questions to answer cold in writing, and some discussion, however limited, is recommended before writing.

The third section, 'Exercises', gives varied opportunities for

INTRODUCTION

written work based on the extract and discussion. In most cases the pupils should be set a selection from these exercises, according to their ability, and the circumstances in which they are used. They require a variety of techniques, including continuous composition, summarising, vocabulary selection, letter writing and so on. Sometimes a group approach has been suggested, but most of the exercises could be undertaken by individual pupils.

It is hoped that the chapters can be used in the order of their presentation as the themes develop one from the other, but there may often be very strong reason for taking a chapter or section of a chapter at a time when it is made relevant by work in social studies say, by events in school or local life, or by class visits forming part of the total course.

In other words, this book, far from replacing the teacher, becomes what the teacher makes of it. If the teacher simply works through, using one section a week, one part a term, making available in class, or in library, or through a school bookshop, the books introduced, then this volume will have served a purpose. If it can be fitted by the teacher or team of teachers, imaginatively and selectively, into a comprehensive course that actively prepares its young people for leaving school and looking at life with maturer eyes, then it will have done all that a school book can honestly hope to do.

JOHN WATTS

Contents

Introduction   vi

PART ONE: HOME AND ABOUT

1 Growing Up

Cider with Rosie LAURIE LEE	1
The Adventures of Huckleberry Finn MARK TWAIN	5
The Taste of Too Much CLIFFORD HANLEY	9

2 The Home (Security and insecurity)

The Only Child JAMES KIRKUP	14
Sons and Lovers D. H. LAWRENCE	17
Pupils' Writings	20

3 The Local Community (Neighbours)

The Limit JOYCE CARY	23
Lark Rise FLORA THOMPSON	27
The Ballad of the Sad Café CARSON MCCULLERS	31

4 Law and Order (Who shall rule?)

Lord of the Flies WILLIAM GOLDING	36
The Persian Expedition XENOPHON; trans. REX WARNER	40
The Death of Grass JOHN CHRISTOPHER	44

PART TWO: WORK AND LEISURE

5 Jobs

Kipps H. G. WELLS	51
The Wheelwright's Shop GEORGE STURT	55
One Day in the Life of Ivan Denisovich ALEXANDER SOLZHENITSYN	59

6 Leisure

Nottingham and the Mining Country D. H. LAWRENCE	64
The Ballad of Billy Rose LESLIE NORRIS	67
Elvin's Rides HAROLD ELVIN	70

CONTENTS

7 Communicating (How can we know?)

Scoop EVELYN WAUGH		75
Death of a Salesman ARTHUR MILLER		77
Except the Lord JOYCE CARY		80

8 Education

The History of Mr Polly H. G. WELLS		84
Hurry on Down JOHN WAIN		88
To Sir, With Love E. R. BRAITHWAITE		93

PART THREE: THE WORLD COMMUNITY

9 The Citizen

The Moon is Down JOHN STEINBECK		99
Serjeant Musgrave's Dance JOHN ARDEN		102
Each His Own Wilderness DORIS LESSING		105

10 Toleration

The Black Madonna MURIEL SPARK		110
The Grapes of Wrath JOHN STEINBECK		114
The Power and the Glory GRAHAM GREENE		117

11 International Relations (Other peoples)

A Pattern of Islands SIR ARTHUR GRIMBLE		122
Shooting an Elephant GEORGE ORWELL		125

12 Responsibilities

Strike the Father Dead JOHN WAIN		130
The Caucasian Chalk Circle BERTHOLT BRECHT		134
The Gospel of Luke trans. J. B. PHILLIPS		136

Notes on Books and Authors   139

List of Plates

		Facing page
1	Growing up *photograph by Ben Johnson*	18
2	The Home—a migrant pea-picker with her two children, U.S.A., 1936 *photograph by Dorothea Lange, taken for the Farm Security Administration, courtesy of the Library of Congress*	19
3	The local community—neighbours *photograph by Ben Johnson*	34
4	Law and order—who shall rule? Speakers' Corner, Hyde Park, London *photograph by Ben Johnson*	35
5	Jobs—combing jute *photograph by Ben Johnson*	66
6	Leisure—Kensington Gardens, London *photograph by Ben Johnson*	67
7	Communications *photograph by Ben Johnson*	82
8	Education ABOVE: A school group, about 1910 *London County Council* BELOW: At a secondary school today *Keystone Press Agency Ltd*	83
9	The citizen—protest march *photograph by Crispin Eurich*	114
10	Toleration—thirteen different nationalities work in this factory, making ballet shoes *Keystone Press Agency Ltd*	115

LIST OF PLATES

11 International relationships—a Tibetan house-father and his 'family' at the British Pestalozzi Children's Village, Sedlescombe, Sussex 130
photograph by Trevor Fry

12 Personal responsibility—a French rescue worker carries an injured child 131
Camera Press Ltd

Acknowledgements

We are grateful to the following for permission to reproduce copyright material:

Geoffrey Bles Ltd for material from *The New Testament in Modern English* translated by J. B. Phillips; The Bodley Head Ltd for material from *To Sir, With Love* by E. R. Braithwaite; The Bodley Head Ltd and Penguin Books Ltd for material from Xenophon's *The Persian Expedition* translated by Rex Warner; Cambridge University Press for material from *The Wheelwright's Shop* by George Sturt; the author's agents for material from *The Death of Grass* by John Christopher, published by Michael Joseph Ltd; The Cresset Press for material from *Death of a Salesman* by Arthur Miller; Curtis Brown Ltd on behalf of the Estate of Joyce Cary for material from *Except the Lord* and *The Limit* by Joyce Cary; Faber and Faber Ltd for material from *Lord of the Flies* by William Golding; Victor Gollancz Ltd for material from *One Day in the Life of Ivan Denisovich* by A. Solzhenitsyn; the author's agents for material from *The Power and the Glory* by Graham Greene, published by William Heinemann Ltd; William Heinemann Ltd and The Viking Press Inc. for material from *The Grapes of Wrath* by John Steinbeck, copyright © 1939 by John Steinbeck; The Hogarth Press Ltd for material from *Cider With Rosie* by Laurie Lee; Hutchinson & Co. Ltd for material from *The Taste of Too Much* by Clifford Hanley; the author's agents for material from *The Only Child* by James Kirkup; the Estate of the late Mrs Frieda Lawrence and Laurence Pollinger Ltd for material from *Sons and Lovers* and *Nottingham and the Mining Countryside* by D. H. Lawrence, published by William Heinemann Ltd; the author's agents for material from *Each His Own Wilderness* by Doris Lessing; Longmans, Green & Co. Ltd for material from *Elvin's Rides* by Harold Elvin; Macmillan & Co. Ltd for material from *Strike the Father Dead* by John Wain; Methuen & Co. Ltd for material from *Serjeant Musgrave's Dance* by John Arden; Methuen & Co. Ltd and the International Copyright Bureau Ltd for material from *The Caucasian Chalk Circle* by Bertholt Brecht translated by John Holmstrom; the author's agents for material from *Ballad of the Sad Café* by Carson McCullers, published by The Cresset Press Ltd; John Murray (Publishers) Ltd for material from *A Pattern of Islands* by Sir Arthur Grimble; the author for 'The Ballad of Billy Rose' by Leslie Norris; Harold Ober Associates Inc. for material from 'The Black Madonna' from *The Go-Away Bird* by Muriel Spark, copyright © 1958 by Muriel Spark; the Estate of the late George Orwell for material from *Shooting an Elephant* by George Orwell, published by Martin Secker & Warburg Ltd; Oxford University Press for material from *Lark Rise* by Flora Thompson; Martin Secker & Warburg Ltd for material from *Hurry On Down* by John Wain; the author's agents for material from *The Moon is Down* by John Steinbeck, and the Executors of H. G. Wells for material from *Kipps* and *The History of Mr Polly* by H. G. Wells.

ACKNOWLEDGEMENTS

The author would also like to thank Anthony Melia and Colin Linsell for their contributions to the book, and Miss Lindsey Braidford for her secretarial work in connection with the manuscript.

One: Home and About

1 Growing Up

¶ 'Why doesn't he grow up?' 'Why doesn't she act her age?' Think of someone you know about whom you might say this. What is it about them that makes you say this?

¶ Growing up involves learning about life and adapting oneself. What sort of thing prevents someone from doing this?

¶ What do you think was the most important lesson learnt in your first ten years? What was the most important one in the years since then?

¶ When would you consider a person to be really grown up?

Cider with Rosie

Peace was here: but I could tell no difference. Our mother returned from far away with excited tales of its madness, of how strangers had stopped and kissed each other in the streets and climbed statues shouting its name. But what was peace anyway? Food tasted the same, pump water was as cold, the house neither fell nor grew larger. Winter came in with a dark, hungry sadness, and the village filled up with unknown men who stood around in their braces and khaki pants, smoking short pipes, scratching their arms, and gazing in silence at the gardens.

I could not believe in this peace at all. It brought no angels or explanations; it had not altered the nature of my days and nights, nor gilded the mud in the yard. So I soon forgot it and went back to my burrowing among the mysteries of indoors and out. The garden still offered its corners of weed, blackened cabbages, its stones and flower-stalks. And the house its areas of hot and cold, dark holes and talking boards, its districts of terror and blessed sanctuary; together with an infinite range of objects and ornaments that folded, fastened, creaked and sighed, opened and shut, tinkled and sang, pinched, scratched, cut, burned, spun, toppled, or fell to pieces. There was also a pepper-smelling cupboard, a ringing cellar, and a humming piano, dry bunches of spiders, colliding brothers, and the eternal comfort of the women.

I was still young enough then to be sleeping with my mother, which to me seemed life's whole purpose. We slept together in the first-floor bedroom on a flock-filled mattress in a bed of brass rods and curtains. Alone, at that time, of all the family, I was her chosen dream companion, chosen from all for her extra love; my right, so it seemed to me.

So in the ample night and the thickness of her hair I consumed my fattened sleep, drowsed and nuzzling to her warmth of flesh, blessed by her bed and safety. From the width of the house and the separation of the day, we two then lay joined alone. That darkness to me was like the fruit of sloes, heavy and ripe to the touch. It was a darkness of bliss and simple languor, when all edges seemed rounded, apt and fitting; and the presence for whom one had moaned and hungered was found not to have fled after all.

My mother, freed from her noisy day, would sleep like a happy child, humped in her nightdress, breathing innocently and making soft drinking sounds in the pillow. In her flights of dream she held me close, like a parachute to her back; or rolled and enclosed me with her great tired body so that I was snug as a mouse in a hayrick.

They were deep and jealous, those wordless nights, as we curled and muttered together, like a secret I held through the waking day which set me above all others. It was for me alone that the night came down, for me the prince of her darkness, when only I would know the huge helplessness of her sleep, her dead face, and her blind bare arms. At dawn, when she rose and stumbled back to the kitchen, even then I was not wholly deserted, but rolled into the valley her sleep had left, lay deep in its smell of lavender, deep on my face to sleep again in the nest she had made my own.

The sharing of her bed at that three-year-old time I expected to last for ever. I had never known, or could not recall, any night spent away from her. But I was growing fast; I was no longer the baby; brother Tony lay in wait in his cot. When I heard the first whispers of moving me to the boys' room, I simply couldn't believe it. Surely my mother would never agree? How could she face night without me?

My sisters began by soothing and flattering; they said, 'You're a grown big man.' 'You'll be sleeping with Harold and Jack,' they said. 'Now what d'you think of that?' What was I supposed to think?—to me it seemed outrageous. I affected a brainstorm and won a few extra nights, my last nights in that downy bed. Then the girls changed their tune: 'It'll only be for a bit. You can come back to Mum later on.' I didn't quite believe them, but Mother was silent, so I gave up the struggle and went.

I was never recalled to my mother's bed again. It was my first betrayal, my first dose of ageing hardness, my first lesson in the gentle, merciless rejection of women. Nothing more was said, and I accepted it. I grew a little tougher, a little colder, and turned my attention more towards the outside world, which by now was emerging visibly through the mist. . . .

The yard and the village manifested themselves at first through magic and fear. Projections of their spirits and of my hallucinations sketched in the first blanks with demons. The thumping of heart-beats which I heard in my head was no longer the unique ticking of a private clock but the marching of monsters coming in from outside. They were creatures of the 'world' and they were coming for me, advancing up the valley with their heads stuck in bread-baskets, grunting to the thump of my blood. I suppose they were a result of early headaches, but I spent anxious days awaiting them. Indefatigable marchers though they were, they never got nearer than the edge of the village.

This was a daylight uneasiness which I shared with no one; but night, of course, held various others about which I was far more complaining—dying candles, doors closed on darkness, faces seen upside-down, night holes in the ground where imagination seethed and sent one shrieking one's chattering head off. There were the Old Men too, who lived in the walls, in floors, and down the lavatory; who watched and judged us and were pitilessly spiteful, and were obviously gods gone mouldy. The Old Men never failed to control us boys, and our sisters conjured them shamelessly, and indeed in a house where no father ruled they were the perfect surrogates.

LAURIE LEE

Questions

1   Laurie could not understand why the village filled with 'unknown men who stood around in their braces' (l. 7). Who do you think they were?

2   How much do we learn about the cottage and its surroundings from this chapter?

3   What does the author mean by 'the width of the house and the separation of the day' (l. 31)?

4 What can we gather from this chapter about Laurie's mother?

5 How did Laurie first know that he would have to leave his mother's bed? Why could he not believe it?

6 What two different methods did the sisters use to persuade Laurie that he wouldn't mind moving?

7 How did Laurie delay the move and why did he eventually agree to it?

8 What did his own heart-beats sound like to Laurie in the days before he slept alone? What did they come to sound like to him afterwards?

9 Who or what were the Old Men?

10 'Our sisters conjured them shamelessly' (l. 91). What does this mean? Why did the girls 'conjure them'?

Implications

11 Laurie Lee recalls the intense early memories of his home, its noises, smells, feelings. What are your own earliest memories of this kind?

12 Why do you think Laurie slept with his mother in the first place? Do you think it is ever advisable for a small child to sleep with its mother?

13 The sisters deceived Laurie. What do you think their motives were? Is it ever right or necessary to deceive a child?

14 In different places Laurie Lee speaks of 'the eternal comfort of the women' (l. 21), and 'the gentle, merciless rejection of women' (l. 68). Is he contradicting himself?

15 'I grew a little tougher, a little colder' (l. 69). Is this process inevitable, to some degree, as a child grows up?

Exercises

16 Write about one of the following:
 a Overcoming an early fear.
 b First lessons in facing the outside world.
 c My first disappointment.
 d Living with brothers and sisters.
 e The dark.

17 Write the dialogue that might have taken place between Mrs Lee and the girls about how to get Laurie to accept the move. It may help if you try improvising this in groups before you attempt writing.

18 List, in the shortest way, your five earliest memories.

19 'That darkness to me was like the fruit of sloes, heavy and ripe to the touch' (l. 32).

This is a striking and original comparison. Compose a similar comparison, in one sentence, for your own early memories of each of the following:
a cupboards.
b bath-time.
c dustbins.
d a light in the dark.
e the attic or cellar or outhouse or shed.

¶ *If you earn any money while still at school, should you hand it over to your parents? Under what conditions would you feel you had to contribute to your parents' needs?*

¶ *When would you feel you had a right not to obey your parents?*

Huckleberry Finn

[A boy, ill-treated and neglected by his father, is adopted by a rich widow. Some time later the father calls unexpectedly on the son.]

I had shut the door to. Then I turned around, and there he was. I used to be scared of him all the time, he tanned me so much. I reckoned I was scared now, too; but in a minute I see I was mistaken. That is, after the first jolt, as you may say, when my breath sort of hitched—he being so unexpected; but right away after, I see I warn't scared of him worth bothering about.

He was most fifty, and he looked it. His hair was long and tangled and greasy, and hung down, and you could see his eyes shining through like he was behind vines. It was all black, no grey; so was his long, mixed-up whiskers. There warn't no colour in his face, where his face showed; it was white; not like another man's white, but a white to make a body sick, a white to make a body's flesh crawl—a tree-toad white, a fish-belly white. As for his clothes—just rags, that was all. He had one ankle resting on t'other knee; the boot on that foot was busted, and two of his toes stuck through, and he worked them now and then. His hat was laying on the floor; an old black slouch with the top caved in, like a lid.

I stood a-looking at him; he set there a-looking at me, with his chair tilted back a little. I set the candle down. I noticed the window was up; so he had clumb in by the shed. He kept a-looking me all over. By-and-by he says:

'Starchy clothes—very. You think you're a good deal of a big-bug, don't you?'

'Maybe I am, maybe I ain't,' I says.

'Don't you give me none o' your lip,' says he. 'You've put on considerble many frills since I been away. I'll take you down a peg before I get done with you. You're educated, too, they say; can read and write. You think you're better'n your father, now, don't you, because he can't? I'll take it out of you. Who told you you might meddle with such hifalut'n foolishness, hey?—who told you you could?'

'The widow. She told me.'

'The widow, hey?—and who told the widow she could put in her shovel about a thing that ain't none of her business?'

'Nobody never told her.'

'Well, I'll learn her how to meddle. And looky here—you drop that school, you hear? I'll learn people to bring up a boy to put on airs over his own father and let on to be better'n what he is. You lemme catch you fooling around that school again, you hear? Your mother couldn't read, and she couldn't write, nuther, before she died. None of the family couldn't, before they died. I can't; and here you're a-swelling yourself up like this. I ain't the man to stand it—you hear? Say—lemme hear you read.'

I took up a book and begun something about General Washington and the wars. When I'd read about a half-minute, he fetched the book a whack with his hand and knocked it across the house. He says:

'It's so. You can do it. I had my doubts when you told me. Now looky here; you stop that putting on frills. I won't have it. I'll lay for you, my smarty; and if I catch you about that school I'll tan you good. First you know you'll get religion, too. I never see such a son.'

He took up a little blue and yaller picture of some cows and a boy, and says:

'What's this?'

'It's something they give me for learning my lessons good.'

He tore it up, and says:

'I'll give you something better—I'll give you a cowhide.'

He set there a-mumbling and a-growling a minute, and then he says:

'Ain't you a sweet-scented dandy, though? A bed; and bedclothes; and a look'n-glass; and a piece of carpet on the floor—and your own father got to sleep with the hogs in the tanyard. I never seen such a son. I bet I'll take some o' these frills out o' you before I'm done with you. Why, there ain't no end to your airs—they say you're rich. Hey?—how's that?'

'They lie—that's how.'

'Looky here—mind how you talk to me; I'm a-standing about all I can stand, now—so don't gimme no sass. I've been in town two days, and I hain't heard nothing but about you bein' rich. I heard about it away down the river, too. That's why I come. You git me that money to-morrow—I want it.'

'I hain't got no money.'

'It's a lie. Judge Thatcher's got it. You git it. I want it.'

'I hain't got no money, I tell you. You ask Judge Thatcher; he'll tell you the same.'

'All right. I'll ask him; and I'll make him pungle, too, or I'll know the reason why. Say—how much you got in your pocket? I want it.'

'I hain't got only a dollar, and I want that to——'

'It don't make no difference what you want it for—you just shell it out.'

He took it and bit it to see if it was good, and then he said he was going down town to get some whisky; said he hadn't had a drink all day. When he had got out on the shed, he put his head in again, and cussed me for putting on frills and trying to be better than him; and when I reckoned he was gone, he came back and put his head in again, and told me to mind about that school, because he was going to lay for me and lick me, if I didn't drop that.

Next day he was drunk, and he went to Judge Thatcher's and bullyragged him and tried to make him give up the money, but he couldn't, and then he swore he'd make the law force him.

MARK TWAIN

Questions

1 Why had Huck been scared of his father before this?

2 As Huck 'stood a-looking at him' (l. 18), how do we know that his feeling about his father is not now one of fear? What is it?

3 What is the father's feeling about his son after they have looked each other over?

4 What reasons does Huck's father give for wanting him to remain illiterate?

5 What were his real reasons for objecting to Huck's being educated?

6 Is there any truth, as far as we can tell in this extract, in the accusation that Huck is 'a-swelling himself up' (l. 42)?

7 What does Huck's father fear will be the next step in his son's road to ruin?

8 What evidence has the father for thinking Huck to be rich?

9 Find two examples of the father's distrust of his son.

10 Why did Huck's father visit him at all?

Implications

11 'Right away after, I see I warn't scared of him worth bothering about' (l. 5). Should a father keep his son or daughter in fear of him? If so, what happens when the father is no longer feared?

12 It is quite common nowadays for a family to find that the children overtake the parents' level of education. What difficulties are likely to be caused by this?

13 What is likely to happen when a son or daughter becomes critical of a parent's appearance or habits?

14 Should a parent have a claim to the income of a teenager?

Exercises

15 Huck Finn tells his story in his own Missouri dialect. Collect ten examples of his dialect, words or phrases, and then write down the nearest expression you can find for each in English.

16 Write a dialogue between a modern parent and a teenage son or daughter on one or more of the matters raised between Huck and his father.

17 Write an account of how you came to realise that someone you had previously feared no longer scared you.

¶ *At what age should a girl be allowed by her parents to come home alone after a dance?*

The Taste of Too Much

[Peter Haddow, a Glasgow boy, is walking home from a school dance.]

He took the path across the waste ground, away from the housing scheme where he lived, and walked up and down streets to pass enough time to convince his sister Christine that he had taken a girl home, because Christine would be waiting at home for a cosy talk about it, and it never crossed his mind not to deceive her. The truth would only annoy her.

As he approached his house he saw two girls standing at the gate. One was Christine. With a small lifting of the spirits, Peter saw that the other was Jean Pynne.

'It's the conquering hero,' Christine said. 'This is my baby brother, Peter.'

'I know,' said Jean Pynne. She was probably the same age as Christine, about twenty. Seeing her seemed to diminish the importance of the dance. She was the legendary Jean Pynne, the fixed standard of comparison in all discussion on feminine beauty between Peter and his friends. She was dark and slender and gorgeous.

Christine tucked her arm into Peter's and leaned on him, and the display of sisterly warmth irritated him mildly because it seemed to signal the end of the conversation with Jean. She's only a girl, after all, Peter chid himself. But it wasn't true.

'Go on talking,' he said, and cleared his throat. 'Go on talking.'

'Come on, I want to hear everything about the Big Romance,' Christine said. Her air of self-conscious ownership was flattering but bothersome.

'There are some things a gentleman doesn't discuss,' he said, and Christine shook him impatiently. Jean Pynne said, 'Well, it's time I was away home. Cheerio.' She hung momentarily on her farewell. Just imagine, Peter thought, his mind racing. Just imagine taking Jean Pynne home. She's standing here talking to me—Jean Pynne. I'll never get the chance again.

'I'll walk you home.'

'What?' Christine was indignant. 'Two in the one night?'

'You must be freezing,' Jean said. It was mere politeness.

'Oh, I'm young and strong.'

'You're the limit,' Christine said. She was annoyed.

'I don't mind.' Jean Pynne laughed doubtfully, and Peter disengaged his arm from Christine's grasp.

'I'm not going to the moon,' he said. 'Women shouldn't be about at this time of the night without protection.'

'Ho, ho,' Christine scoffed. 'You get straight back here. I'm putting the kettle on now.' Peter fell into step beside Jean Pynne, wondering how it could have been so easy. They walked in silence, awkwardly, looking straight ahead.

'Did you enjoy the dance?' Jean asked him. Was there a hint of condescension in her voice? Peter shrugged.

'It was all right. Dancing is a rather lowbrow pastime, actually. I'm more of the intellectual type. You know, chess, Hindu philosophy, all that trash.'

Jean gave a delicious little giggle. Her cheek was impossibly smooth and transparent and her teeth flashed white in the lamplight. 'You talk funny,' she said.

'It's because I'm adolescent,' Peter told her. 'I'm precociously immature. I talk too much. Sometimes I have to listen to myself making dopey jokes when I wish I would shut up or say something else. It's a disease.'

... Jean laughed again, helplessly, and put one of her arms in his to support her. Peter squeezed tight on it and imprisoned it as they walked on.

'How did you ever get home?' Jean asked him, '—if you've been talking like this to somebody else?'

'Can I talk seriously to you?'

'If you like.'

'I didn't see any girl home from the school dance. I didn't have the nerve. I talk a lot, but I'm a coward.'

'That's a shame,' said Jean. 'Imagine how the girls feel that nobody took home. It's awful, you don't know how awful it is.'

This novel view of the situation startled Peter, who had hoped for warm sympathy.

'I didn't think of that,' he admitted. 'I suppose I'm a rat, as well as a coward.'

'I would probably be just as bad, if I was a boy,' Jean said.

'Ah, it's a terrible business, sex,' Peter said, and added, 'I don't mean sex, like that. I mean, having two sexes in the world. It truly baffles me. I bet you're fed up listening to me.'

'No, honestly, don't be silly.'

'Well, half the people are one sex and half the people are the other sex. *All the time*, I mean. When you think of all the trouble it causes. What if everybody was the same sex most of the time, and then just a different sex occasionally, or if there was no sex most of the time and just sex now and then, like dressing up for Hallowe'en. Do you know this? I've started to talk absolute nonsense again.'

'I don't quite get it.'

'Good, I don't either. But it truly baffles me anyway. How do I *know* some girl wanted me to take her home from the dance? If some girl did. There should be some better system. I don't even know what to say to a girl. I talk a lot but I don't know. I don't know what they're thinking.'

'They're just ordinary, they just think ordinary things.'

Peter gave a short, bitter laugh.

'All right,' he said, 'say I had taken some girl home from the dance——'

'What's her name?'

'She hasn't got a name,' he blustered. 'It's just a hypothesis. So I take her home. I still don't know what she's thinking, and she doesn't know what I'm thinking. Does she want me to kiss her good night? The way we talk in the class, we're all big guys, men of the world, we've done everything, but that's what it boils down to, does this girl want us to kiss her good night? And how do you start?'

'I don't know,' Jean said helplessly. 'It's up to the boy.'

'Well, do I break off in the middle of a sentence about trigonometry and woof! Probably land in her eye, or her ear,' he added glumly.

'It can't be as difficult as that, if she likes you. It shouldn't be difficult for you, anyway. Most of the boys that used to take me home couldn't say anything at all, and neither could I. You can talk.'

Peter brightened at once. 'Could I have talked you into kissing me good night—if I was taking you home from a dance?'

'What is this leading up to?' Jean looked sideways at him and saw him shake his head and saw his bony baffled face and felt that she had been elected to the status of a woman of the world. How old was Peter? And how was a sophisticate supposed to act in this situation? They had reached her gate, and Peter still had her arm in his.

'There's nothing to it,' Jean said shakily. She raised her free arm to touch his cheek and turn his face towards her, and kissed him lightly on the mouth. 'See?'

'Hey,' Peter said. 'You kissed me.'

Jean disengaged her arm firmly.

'It was just a demonstration.' She opened the gate and moved to the inside of it. 'Now you'll know next time.' She giggled in spite of her determination to be calm and controlled. Peter was standing with his arms hanging limply by his sides.

'Well, good night,' he said. Jean ran up to the front door, but he called after her, and she turned round.

'Thank you!' he called in a whisper. Jean waved her arm and vanished into the house. Inside the front door she stopped to find that she was blushing and breathless. Soft as a jelly, she accused herself in irritation. For God's sake, I'm nineteen.

CLIFFORD HANLEY

Questions

1 Why does Peter walk away from his home and then walk up and down?

2 Why does Peter think that his sister would only be annoyed by the truth?

3 In what way has Peter regarded Jean Pynne up to now?

4 What is meant by 'she hung momentarily on her farewell' (l. 28)? Why do you think Jean did this?

5 What does Christine mean by 'two in the one night' (l. 33)? Why is she indignant?

6 What is meant by 'a hint of condescension in her voice' (l. 45)? Why did Peter suspect there might be one?

7 What caused Jean and Peter to link arms?

8 How can we tell that Peter fears Jean will find him boring?

9 How have Peter and his male friends been boastful at school?

10 Why is Peter's final remark 'Thank you'?

Implications

11 'I'm more of the intellectual type' (l. 48). How seriously do you think Peter means this?

12 Why does Peter confess to Jean that he has not taken anyone home from the dance?

13　How can you tell that Peter is unused to walking girls home?

14　' "There's nothing to it," Jean said shakily' (l. 114). What does the word 'shakily' imply?

15　Was it wise of Jean to allow a boy two years younger than herself to take an interest in her?

Exercises

16　Write a diary entry that either Peter or Jean might have made that evening.

17　Write down the conversation that Peter has with his sister Christine on his return.

18　Give an account of your first dance.

Discussion and Writing

Photograph 1 (facing page 18)

Whose point of interest is the photographer sharing?

What is the boy on the left doing?

What class of cricket would you say was being played?

What other parts might the boys be allowed to take in cricket of this kind? When would they be able to join the game itself?

Write about 'Father's sporting days' or, 'The Family Weekend'.

2 *The Home* *(Security and insecurity)*

¶ *For the most part we take home for granted—until something goes wrong. What sort of upset could most easily throw your own home life into confusion?*

¶ *If there were a serious accident that upset your normal home life, how would this affect your work?*

¶ *What can you remember most vividly about starting school as an infant? Can you remember not wanting to go back to school?*

¶ *What do you still like best about getting home after being out all day?*

The Only Child

The trying times I had at the Infants' School made me love my home and my mother and father more than ever. I don't think I actually loved them more—that was not possible, and in any case 'love' signified nothing then—but I began to realise how much they meant to me, how sad it was to be separated from them, even for a few hours a day, and how awful it would be, in this terrible new world of school and violence, if they were not there at all.

Coupled with my anxieties at school was the fear that, when I returned home at dinner-time or tea-time I should find them gone, the house locked up and deserted, or, even worse, occupied by strangers who would insist on adopting me as their son. So immediately after lessons were over, I would not linger in the classroom 'sucking up to teacher' as the 'teacher's pets' did; nor would I play in the school yard with top and whip or bat and ball as so many children did. I would take to my heels and run home as fast as I could. Sometimes the older children, seeing how eager I was to get home, would ambush me outside the school gates and keep me prisoner for five or ten minutes. I learned to submit without a struggle: there was no point in offering any resistance.

If I ran all the way, I could be home in two minutes, and I would arrive at the back door panting and happy. My mother always had dinner ready for me, and it was a sad dinner-time for me when there was no rice pudding, my favourite dish. On cold, winter days we would have our dinner on trays by the fireside, while the wind roared outside and rain lashed the window-panes and the sea boomed beyond the house-tops. They were happy, cosy, intimate meals. It was a great treat to have dinner or tea by the blazing fire, with our feet up on the sparkling brass fender of the whitewashed hearth. But it made going back to school even harder. If there was dense fog outside, I would sit by the fire in my slippers until the last possible minute, listening to the glum blasts of the foghorn and the wailing sirens of fog-bound ships outside the harbour. Then, with a high-pitched urgency, the school bell would begin to ring, and I would scramble into my coat and cap and outdoor shoes, cover my mouth and nose with my muffler, and dash out into the dead, damp fog. The school bell, rung by the old caretaker in his shirt-sleeves and bowler hat, filled me with anguish and excitement, and as I ran along, carefully avoiding the black cracks in the pavement, my steps kept time—had to keep time with it. These were two magical devices I had invented to keep trouble away. Another was to cross the toecap of my shoe with spit whenever I saw a white horse. Picking up coal was also lucky, and it was advisable to cross one's fingers if a black cat ran across one's path.

One morning I was in such a hurry to get to school—I had left it rather late, and the bell was ringing maddeningly, as if it knew I was in a fix—my mother put my shoes on the wrong feet while I was struggling into my coat. All morning my feet felt uncomfortable, but I did not realise what was wrong until I got home for dinner and told my mother how my feet hurt. She told me she'd put my shoes on the wrong feet, and we had a good laugh. But it was the first time I'd ever known her make a mistake, and there was an undercurrent of uncertainty in my laughter.

Yes, it was wonderful to be at home, and not at school, and whenever I was in the house I would look at things with an intent, almost morbid thoroughness, as if I might never see them again. The patterns on the tablecloths, the plates, the wallpaper, the linoleum and on our big Axminster carpet in the front room—how proud my mother was of it, and looked after it so well that as I write now, my feet still rest on its almost undimmed, magical splendour—all these I studied with obsessional intensity until I knew every colour, every repetition, every convolution of their extraordinary designs. The carpet was the most interesting of all. It had all kinds of peculiar abstract shapes woven into it, and I would try hard to rationalise them: one was a tram car, several of them were cakes or sweets, one was a tortoise, another a castle, another a giant beetle. I spent hours poring over those patterns, trying to extract the hidden meaning which I was sure lay behind them. But they were very mysterious—even my mother and father couldn't tell me what they meant.

JAMES KIRKUP

Questions

1 What were the boy's strongest feelings about school already?

2 What did the boy fear most about being away from home?

3 'I learned to submit' (l. 18). What do we gather from this about what had happened previously? Why does he now offer no resistance?

4 To emphasise the joy and comfort of being indoors at dinner-time James Kirkup mentions certain things happening outside. What are they and how do they give this emphasis?

5 What details show the boy's reluctance to set off for school?

6 What does he mean by 'anguish and excitement' (l. 37)?

7 What fear is shown in the boy's 'undercurrent of uncertainty' (l. 52) in his laughter over the shoes?

8 What does James Kirkup mean by 'morbid thoroughness' (l. 55)? Why did the boy study the details of his home with this 'intent, almost morbid thoroughness'?

9 What did he find specially interesting about the carpet?

10 Is there anything to show that James Kirkup was more tied to his home than most other children?

Implications

11 Can you remember not wanting to go to school at this boy's age? What would you suggest to a parent whose small child does not want to go to school? Have you had experience of this with younger brothers or sisters?

12 James Kirkup was an only child. Does a child in a larger family find it any easier to leave the home circle?

13 When, if ever, do you think you will no longer need to turn to your parents for anything?

14 What is the most important thing that your parents have provided for you? What, in turn, do you think will be the most important thing to provide for your own children?

Exercises

15 Write about either (*a*) your first experience of being away from home; or (*b*) your earliest memories of school.

16 List in order of importance the things you would have missed most if away from home as a small child. Then list what you would miss most if away now. How, if at all, do your lists differ?

17 Write a letter to a brother or sister who is away from home, telling him of all the things that he misses and would most like to hear about.

¶ *If one of your parents were seriously ill, how would this affect life at home?*

Sons and Lovers

Morel was rather a heedless man, careless of danger. So he had endless accidents. Now, when Mrs Morel heard the rattle of an empty coal-cart cease at her entry-end, she ran into the parlour to look, expecting almost to see her husband seated in the wagon, his face grey under his dirt, his body limp and sick with some hurt or other. If it were he, she would run out to help.

About a year after William went to London, and just after Paul had left school, before he got work, Mrs Morel was upstairs and her son was painting in the kitchen—he was very clever with his brush—
10 when there came a knock at the door. Crossly he put down his brush to go. At the same moment his mother opened a window upstairs and looked down.

A pit-lad in his dirt stood on the threshold.

'Is this Walter Morel's?' he asked.

'Yes,' said Mrs Morel. 'What is it?'

But she had guessed already.

'Your mester's got hurt,' he said.

'Eh, dear me!' she exclaimed. 'It's a wonder if he hadn't, lad. And what's he done this time?'

20 'I don't know for sure, but it's 'is leg somewhere. They ta'ein' 'im ter th' 'ospital.'

'Good gracious me!' she exclaimed. 'Eh, dear, what a one he is! There's not five minutes of peace, I'll be hanged if there is! His thumb's nearly better, and now—Did you see him?'

'I seed him at th' bottom. An' I seed 'em bring 'im up in a tub, an' 'e wor in a dead faint. But he shouted like anythink when Doctor Fraser examined him i' th' lamp cabin—an' cossed an' swore, an' said 'e wor goin' to be ta'en whoam—'e worn't goin' ter th' 'ospital.'

The boy faltered to an end.

'He would want to come home, so that I can have all the bother. Thank you, my lad. Eh, dear, if I'm not sick—sick and surfeited, I am!'

She came downstairs. Paul had mechanically resumed his painting.

'And it must be pretty bad if they've taken him to the hospital,' she went on. 'But what a careless creature he is! Other men don't have all these accidents. Yes, he would want to put all the burden on me. Eh, dear, just as we were getting easy a bit at last. Put those things away, there's no time to be painting now. What time is there a train? I know I s'll have to go trailing to Keston. I s'll have to leave that bedroom.'

'I can finish it,' said Paul.

'You needn't. I shall catch the seven o'clock back, I should think. Oh, my blessed heart, the fuss and commotion he'll make! And those granite setts at Tinder Hill—he might well call them kidney pebbles—they'll jolt him almost to bits. I wonder why they can't mend them, the state they're in, an' all the men as go across in that ambulance. You'd think they'd have a hospital here. The men bought the ground, and, my sirs, there'd be accidents enough to keep it going. But no, they must trail them ten miles in a slow ambulance to Nottingham. It's a crying shame! Oh, and the fuss he'll make! I know he will! I wonder who's with him. Barker, I s'd think. Poor beggar, he'll wish himself anywhere rather. But he'll look after him, I know. Now there's no telling how long he'll be stuck in that hospital—and won't he hate it! But if it's only his leg it's not so bad.'

All the time she was getting ready. Hurriedly taking off her bodice, she crouched at the boiler while the water ran slowly into her lading-can.

'I wish this boiler was at the bottom of the sea!' she exclaimed, wriggling the handle impatiently. She had very handsome, strong arms, rather surprising on a smallish woman.

Paul cleared away, put on the kettle, and set the table.

'There isn't a train till four-twenty,' he said. 'You've time enough.'

'Oh no, I haven't!' she cried, blinking at him over the towel as she wiped her face.

2

'Yes, you have. You must drink a cup of tea at any rate. Should I come with you to Keston?'

'Come with me? What for, I should like to know? Now, what have I to take him? Eh, dear! His clean shirt—and it's a blessing it is clean. But it had better be aired. And stockings—he won't want them—and a towel, I suppose; and handkerchiefs. Now what else?'

'A comb, a knife and fork and spoon,' said Paul. His father had been in the hospital before.

'Goodness knows what sort of state his feet were in,' continued Mrs Morel, as she combed her long brown hair that was fine as silk, and was touched now with grey. 'He's very particular to wash himself to the waist, but below he thinks doesn't matter. But there, I suppose they see plenty like it.'

Paul had laid the table. He cut his mother one or two pieces of very thin bread and butter.

'Here you are,' he said, putting her cup of tea in her place.

'I can't be bothered!' she exclaimed crossly.

'Well, you've got to, so there, now it's put out ready,' he insisted.

So she sat down and sipped her tea, and ate a little, in silence. She was thinking.

In a few minutes she was gone, to walk the two and a half miles to Keston Station. All the things she was taking him she had in her bulging string bag. Paul watched her go up the road between the hedges—a little, quick-stepping figure—and his heart ached for her, that she was thrust forward again into pain and trouble.

D. H. LAWRENCE

Questions

1   What makes it clear that Mrs Morel half expected an accident? Why should she have done?

2   The pit-lad is not quite certain of what happened to Morel. How much does he know for sure?

3   'There's not five minutes of peace' (l. 23). 'He would want to come home' (l. 30). How would you describe these reactions of Mrs Morel to her husband's accident?

4   Why does Mrs Morel tell Paul to put his paints away?

5   What is there to show that Mrs Morel felt pity and anxiety for her husband as well as annoyance?

6   How can we tell that Paul is concerned for his mother?

7   In the same way, how can we tell that Mrs Morel is concerned for Paul?
8   What reaction does Paul show to his father's accident?
9   Why does Mrs Morel call Barker a 'poor beggar' (l. 52)?
10 What evidence is there in the passage for saying that Mrs Morel's life was not an easy one?

Implications

11 Do you find it credible that a person can feel annoyed with someone they love, and at the same time feel pity and anxiety as Mrs Morel did? Think of examples of your own.
12 Was Morel selfish in wanting to be brought home rather than to be taken to hospital? Was he being unreasonable?
13 Was Mrs Morel selfish to blame him for wanting to come home?
14 Does a mother hold the most responsible place in the home? It may help you if you consider the effects upon the family that might follow the father's injury, and those that might result from the mother being taken to hospital.
15 Paul offered to finish a bedroom and make some tea. Should a son be expected to help in the home normally? Should a daughter? Should their contributions be equal?

Exercises

16 Write about a crisis in the family, catching the reactions of all involved.
17 D. H. Lawrence reproduces the Nottinghamshire speech of the pit-lad. Rewrite what he said as if spoken by a boy of your own district.
18 Make a list of things you might need to take to someone who has been taken to hospital in an emergency.

Pupils' Writings

Sometimes the writing of your own classmates can throw light on your own. The following two pieces, written in school, are included not as models of literature, but to provoke thought and discussion about differences in style when honest attempts are made to record experiences. Both pieces were written in response to the extract from *Sons and Lovers* and discussion of family crises.

ANTHONY (14) Mr Pitch returned home after seeing his wife in hospital, He entered the living room where his children were playing with one of the grimest faces the children had ever seen.
The eldest child John asked from the other side of the room, 'How is she Dad,' Mr Pitch said nothing in reply, he just sat in his chair near the fire, and lit his pipe. The children didn't say a thing untill the father told them there mothers condition.
'The Nurse said she'd be better in a week or two but she'll still have to stay in bed for another two weeks so as to let the knee set proper like.'
John asked 'Does that mean we make our own breakfast Dad.'
Mr Pitch replyed looking at his eldest daughter. 'I think Mary can do that John'
Mary was quite a clever girl even if she was the daughter of a laborer. She had come top in her Houscraft Exam so she would have no trouble in making the breakfast and Tea, even if her English Essays were of a low standard.
When the Home help came the children never used to like her because she'd always complne about the state the house was in, But the children didn't argue with her about that, because she made such nice cakes they'd have to go without them if they made her cross.

COLIN (15) The sun streaked through the cool shade of the great oak leaves. I leaned lazily against the new wall. It was the last day of my holiday and I had nothing to do but to watch my father, my uncle and Mr Taylor talk about the new red brick wall that was in the final stage before completion. Mr Taylor had commissioned my uncle to build the wall and this was their main topic of talk. The sun was hot and the flies swung lazily around my head as I picked small pieces of cement out of the wall.
Mr Taylor's wife and daughter came out to join us. They talked for a while and then decided to return to the house. Suddenly Mr Taylor collapsed onto the wet grass, I ran over, my uncle and father were feeling his pulse. I stood there amazed—he seemed so alive but now he was so still. I wondered what was wrong with him, a broken leg, heat stroke, what was wrong.

It seemed that I was struck dumb. I just couldn't bring myself to ask. His daughter was standing over the prostrate figure white and shaking. His wife made a pathetic sight half crying and running around in circles. She burst off to the pub opposite and brought back a bottle of rum. Pushing my uncle aside she pressed the bottle to his lips but with no response, she screamed at him incoherently and my uncle pulled her off the body. Neighbours had arrived and took the mother and daughter back to their house, both in a severe state of shock. My father phoned the ambulance and my uncle brought out the village policeman, leaving me alone with a white and still Mr Taylor who didn't care about the sun or the flies anymore, a rather dead Mr Taylor.

Questions and Exercises

1 *a* How has Anthony conveyed the father's concern for wife and family?
b How has he shown the family's pride and loyalty?
c What details seem to you most true to life?

2 *a* What sort of feeling, or atmosphere, does Colin create in the first paragraph? What details have built this up?
b What details convey the confusion following Mr Taylor's death?
c How does Colin convey his own sense of horror?

3 What differences are there in the ways the two pieces have been written?

4 Put yourself in the position of the teacher marking this work. What comment would you write at the end of each composition and what, if anything, would you correct?

Discussion and Writing

Photograph No. 2 (facing page 19)

This woman is a migrant farm-worker in the United States. What do you think is on her mind? What might she have in common with Mrs Morel?

Write about this woman, or any worried mother.

3 The Local Community *(Neighbours)*

¶ How often have you been warned of what the neighbours will say? Why should it matter what the neighbours say?

¶ What sort of thing causes bad feeling among your neighbours, and what causes good feeling?

¶ When have you or your family found neighbours a help or comfort?

¶ Have you ever been aware of a strong feeling common to everyone around you? Whom or what was the feeling directed towards?

The Limit

It is a shopping street with lights at intervals. As they change, traffic is turned on and off as by a tap. First there is vacancy from pavement to pavement, then a rush from both sides—solid blocks of traffic charging like tanks and, like tanks at the charge, getting quickly out of line.

At this time in the morning young men and women are at work and the pavements are crowded with parents and grandparents doing their household shopping—serious and anxious people in serious clothes. They meet only briefly, for a few short pregnant words on grave matters, children and prices. The children are all young, below school age—they weave in and out of the slow, dark streams of shoppers. They are meeting friends on their own eye level, chasing each other, carrying out various experiments in locomotion such as hopping on one leg, swinging around a lamp-post, pacing carefully on the joints between kerbstones, or walking backwards.

The dogs, at the lowest level, are also paying attention chiefly to each other: their noses point warily about inquiring, seeking, recording; they sidle out of doorways as if from ambush; absorbed in a lamp-post they do not even notice feet, they dodge away at the very last moment; they catch sight of a strange nose that has suddenly projected itself from behind a string bag full of potatoes, and stand with rigid tail and every muscle taut in the question, friend or enemy; they dash wildly off down side streets on some private recollection of the most urgent importance.

The relation between the three levels is one of responsible authority mixed with affection: parents hastily snatch up a child's hand to steer it in the right direction; their gestures say plainly that this is no world to wander in. Children shout peremptory advice at dogs or drag them by the collar from dangerous acquaintances.

A small boy of about four in a red and white jersey stands at the kerb holding a black mongrel puppy by a piece of string tied to its collar. The puppy has a singularly large head, and feet which seem too heavy for its insignificant body. As it tosses its head and tries to bite its string, two children, girl and boy, rather smaller than its owner, desert a perambulator to play with it. Greatly flattered, it twists its neck sideways and turns up its eyes in an affected manner, then throws its front legs about and cavorts like the lion in the royal arms. The children try to tickle it; it pretends to bite them and they squeal. The boy in the striped jersey looks down with watchful but benevolent condescension.

The puppy, growing more excited and still more anxious to please, attempts a more brilliant romp, falls over its own tail and breaks the string. It wriggles upright again and runs backwards into the road, fortunately empty.

The boy with the jersey dives to catch the loose end of the string. The puppy gambols farther off, the lights change and the traffic comes on with a rush—a lorry and a car hoot together. The boy tries to shoo the puppy towards the opposite pavement, but it cavorts sideways. The child makes a sharp turn to head it off and this brings him back in front of the traffic from the nearest light. A sports model, renowned in all the advertisements for its acceleration, has come away with a rush. It strikes the boy somewhere in the back, whirls him around and picks him up on the mudguard.

He makes no sound at all; it is as though a small bundle of coloured clothes has suddenly appeared in the trough of the guard. Brakes and tyres scream, the car stops, shuddering against the kerb, and the bundle slides off and collapses into itself on the roadway exactly like empty garments—limp and soft. In a moment there is a crowd, a policeman holding the ring. A young doctor, or perhaps medical student, kneels down to examine the child—he is quite dead.

The neighbourhood is poor, the car expensive—the crowd is hostile. The women are especially angry. A powerful matron at the back, her bare arms red with work, a man's felt hat balanced on her thick grey hair as if to express her mastery in life, is shouting something about bloody murderers—don't let 'em get away with it.

The motorist is well aware of his danger. At each new shout he looks round nervously; his round, plump face is shining with sweat, his hands fidget with his cap and coat, both of the gayest check.

First he takes off his cap as if feeling that this is only proper in the presence of death. Then, when the policeman questions him, he puts it on again as if to show that he has no reason to humble himself before the law.

The policeman, a tall, bottle-shouldered man, also very young, with a singularly blank face, the face of authority exaggerated by a sense of the occasion, writes carefully and slowly in his notebook. He might be filling in a census form.

At last he turns to the crowd and asks for witnesses—but it appears that no one present has seen the accident. And the question seems only to make the women more angry; they are tired of these slow preliminaries, they are shouting for immediate vengeance.

The young man is terrified, his shaking fingers button and unbutton his coat—the confused idea of making it less conspicuous is followed by a fear that he may seem to be preparing for flight. He looks round the circle of muttering and screaming women and tries to make them understand that he could not have avoided the accident, but not a word can be heard, and his fear, his apologetic grimaces, his fumbling hands also enrage the crowd. It makes a surge forward at some new pressure from behind, and actually touches him. He shrinks against the policeman who stretches out his arm in a commanding and protective manner. But even as he does so he too receives a push in the back which nearly unseats his helmet.

Another wave of pressure goes through the mass and now someone at the back of the ring is shouting, 'Make way there.' The ring opens and a small, pale woman, perhaps forty, perhaps fifty years old, is thrust forward by the woman in the hat. Her triumphant gesture says plainly, 'Here you are—this will finish the talk.' The clamour falters for a moment and the young man's rapid urgent speech breaks through, 'But I couldn't help it—I was just——'

The pale little woman, now also in front of the crowd, interrupts him. 'That's right.'

This produces a complete silence. The policeman puts his helmet straight and so recovers his dignity. He turns with his notebook at the ready. 'Yes, m'am?'

'It wasn't his fault—it wasn't anybody's fault,' the little woman says in a high thin voice.

'You saw it, did you?'

She shakes her head and says, 'No, I was in the shop—I couldn't see anything.'

HOME AND ABOUT

110 'Then how do you know it wasn't anybody's fault?'
'He was my boy.'
Everybody stares at her with amazement and confusion—it is as though she has spoken in Chinese. But she is not at all disconcerted. For the first time she looks at the child's body huddled in the dust, and she says even more loudly, 'No, it wasn't nobody's fault.'
The policeman and the motorist gaze at her still as if she is mad. But the women are already going away. They understand why she doesn't want to blame anybody—she can't take any more bitterness.

JOYCE CARY

Questions

1 How does the author suggest that pedestrians and drivers are at war with each other?
2 What are the three levels of life on the pavements?
3 Why are the shoppers 'serious and anxious' (l. 8)?
4 What is the meaning of 'authority mixed with affection' (l. 26)? How does this show in the adults, and how in the children?
5 What has made the boy's puppy especially frisky?
6 'The crowd is hostile' (l. 61). What special reason have they for disliking the driver even before the accident?
7 Pick out three details that show the driver's confusion and embarrassment.
8 Why could the crowd not really have known whether the driver was to blame or not?
9 Why could the mother not know whether the driver was to blame or not?
10 Why, after all their anger, do the women leave the motorist and go away?

Implications

11 Was any one person responsible for the boy's death?
12 What could have been done to prevent the accident?
13 Why were the women so eager to attack the motorist?
14 What practical help could any of the women in the crowd have given the mother, then or later?

THE LOCAL COMMUNITY

Exercises

15 Make written statements for the police describing the accident
a as if you were a pedestrian eye-witness,
b as if you were the motorist.
In each case try and stick to the facts as as each person would know them.

16 Write out a list of safety rules for pedestrians in a busy shopping area like this.

17 Describe how something that happened in your own neighbourhood aroused strong and united feeling among neighbours.

¶ *What is meant by 'keeping up with the Joneses'?*

¶ *If your friends had subscribed to a charity fund, would you feel you had to keep up with them by giving a similar amount? Would you feel you were letting them down if you did not subscribe?*

Lark Rise

[*Lark Rise* is an autobiographical account of life in an Oxfordshire hamlet at the end of the nineteenth century.]

Up to the middle of the 'eighties the hamlet had taken little interest in the Royal House. The Queen and the Prince and Princess of Wales were sometimes mentioned, but with little respect and no affection. 'The old Queen', as she was called, was supposed to have shut herself up in Balmoral Castle with a favourite servant named John Brown and to have refused to open Parliament when Mr Gladstone begged her to. The Prince was said to be leading a gay life, and the dear, beautiful Princess, afterwards Queen Alexandra, was celebrated only for her supposed make-up.

10   By the middle of the decade a new spirit was abroad and had percolated to the hamlet. The Queen, it appeared, had reigned fifty years. She had been a good queen, a wonderful queen, she was soon to celebrate her Jubilee, and, still more exciting, they were going to celebrate it, too, for there was going to be a big 'do' in which three villages would join for tea and sports and dancing and fireworks in the park of a local magnate. Nothing like it had ever been known before.

As the time drew nearer, the Queen and her Jubilee became the chief topic of conversation. The tradesmen gave lovely coloured portraits of her in her crown and Garter ribbon on their almanacks, most of which were framed at home and hung up in the cottages. Jam could be bought in glass jugs adorned with her profile in hobnails and inscribed '1837 to 1887. Victoria the Good', and, underneath, the national catchword of the moment: 'Peace and Plenty'. The newspapers were full of the great achievements of her reign: railway travel, the telegraph, Free Trade, exports, progress, prosperity, Peace: all these blessings, it appeared, were due to her inspiration.

Of most of these advantages the hamlet enjoyed but Esau's share; but, as no one reflected upon this, it did not damp the general enthusiasm. 'Fancy her reigning fifty years, the old dear, her' they said, and bought paper banners inscribed 'Fifty Years, Mother, Wife, and Queen' to put inside their window panes. 'God Bless Her. Victoria the Good. The Mother of Her People.'

Then there were rumours of a subscription fund. The women of England were going to give the Queen a Jubilee present, and, wonder of wonders, the amount given was not to exceed one penny. 'Of course we shall give,' they said proudly. 'It'll be our duty an' our pleasure.' And when the time came for the collections to be made they had all of them their pennies ready. Bright new ones in most cases, for, although they knew the coins were to be converted into a piece of plate before reaching Her Majesty, they felt that only new money was worthy of the occasion.

The ever-faithful, ever-useful clergyman's daughter collected the pence. Thinking, perhaps, that the day after pay-day would be most convenient, she visited Lark Rise on a Saturday, and Laura, at home from school, was clipping the garden hedge when she heard one neighbour say to another: 'I want a bucket of water, but I can't run round to the well till Miss Ellison's been for the penny.'

'Lordy, dear!' ejaculated the other. 'Why, she's been an' gone this quarter of an hour. She's a-been to my place. Didn't she come to yourn?'

The first speaker, a Mrs Parker, flushed to the roots of her hair. She was a woman whose husband had recently had an accident afield and was still in hospital. There were no insurance benefits then, and it was known she was having a hard struggle to keep her home going; but she had her penny ready and was hurt, terribly hurt, by the suspicion that she had been purposely passed over.

'I s'pose, because I be down on me luck, she thinks I ain't worth a penny,' she cried, and went in and banged the door.

'There's temper for you!' the other woman exclaimed to the world at large and went about her own business. But Laura was distressed. She had seen Mrs Parker's expression and could imagine how her pride was hurt. She, herself, hated to be pitied. But what could she do about it?

She went to the gate. Miss Ellison had finished collecting and was crossing the allotments on her way home. Laura would just have time to run the other way round and meet her at the stile. After a struggle with her own inward shrinking which lasted about two minutes, but was ridiculously intense, she ran off on her long, thin legs, and popped up, like a little jack-in-the-box, on the other side of the stile which the lady was gathering up her long frilly skirts to mount.

'Oh, please, Miss Ellison, you haven't been to Mrs Parker's, and she's got her penny all ready and she wants the Queen to have it so much.'

'But, Laura,' said the lady loftily, surprised at such interference, 'I did not intend to call upon Mrs Parker to-day. With her husband in hospital, I know she has no penny to spare, poor soul.'

But, although somewhat quelled, Laura persisted: 'But she's got it all polished up and wrapped in tissue paper, Miss Ellison, and 'twill hurt her feelings most awful if you don't go for it, Miss Ellison.'

At that, Miss Ellison grasped the situation and retraced her steps, keeping Laura by her side and talking to her as to another grown-up person.

FLORA THOMPSON

Questions

1 What was the 'new spirit' (l. 10) that reached the hamlet by the middle of the decade?

2 'Peace and Plenty' (l. 24).
 a What examples does the author give of Victorian achievements?
 b What does she mean by 'Of most of these advantages the hamlet enjoyed but Esau's share' (l. 29)?

3 When the women of the hamlet saved their pennies for the Queen they tried to find bright new ones. In a way they knew this was pointless, so why did they bother?

4 What phrase suggests that the clergyman's daughter often performed the tasks of visiting and collecting?

5 Why did Miss Ellison not collect Mrs Parker's penny?

6 Why was Mrs Parker offended? What was her reaction to learning that Miss Ellison had left her out?

7 What was the attitude of her neighbours to Mrs Parker's reaction?

8 Why was Laura so anxious for Miss Ellison to return and call on Mrs Parker?

9 Why did Laura have 'inward shrinking' (l. 69) at what she proposed to do?

10 Why do you think Miss Ellison started talking to Laura 'as to another grown-up person' (l. 85)?

Implications

11 When Mrs Parker went in and banged her door, her neighbour 'went about her own business' (l. 62). Should Laura have minded her own business too?

12 How far was Mrs Parker trying to keep up her appearances, how far anxious not to let her neighbours down? Was she being proud, or was she keeping her self-respect? Was she to blame for any of this?

13 Mrs Parker had no insurance benefits. Now that we have them are people likely to be any more or less neighbourly than these villagers were in Lark Rise?

14 Is it useful to have someone in the neighbourhood who will organise things in the way that Miss Ellison seems to have done? Who is it likely to be in your district? What difficulties may such an organiser face?

Exercises

15 Describe an occasion when you found it difficult to decide between going to someone's help and minding your own business.

16 Describe someone you know to be a good neighbour and another who you think makes a bad neighbour.

17 Tell of any part you have played in raising money in your neighbourhood.

18 Write a letter to someone who is coming to live in your neighbourhood explaining what you think they will like about it and what they should be careful about.

19 Design and word a handbill to be printed and distributed locally appealing for a fund such as Oxfam, UNICEF, or a local charity.

¶ *Most people at some time have been wrongly suspected of something. What does it feel like when other people are convinced that you are guilty while you know you are innocent?*

¶ *Have you ever felt able to do something in a group that you would not have done by yourself? When have you felt proud of the outcome and when ashamed?*

The Ballad of the Sad Café

[*The Ballad of the Sad Café* is a short novel about the relationships of a group of people in an American country town. It centres around Miss Amelia's store, for a brief period turned into the town's only café.]

Miss Amelia came down at about dawn, as usual. She washed her head at the pump and very shortly set about her business. Later in the morning she saddled her mule and went to see about her property, planted with cotton, up near the Fork Falls Road. By noon, of course, everybody had heard about the hunchback who had come to the store in the middle of the night. But no one as yet had seen him. The day soon grew hot and the sky was a rich, midday blue. Still no one had laid an eye on this strange guest. A few people remembered that Miss Amelia's mother had had a half-sister—but there was some difference of opinion as to whether she had died or had run off with a tobacco stringer. As for the hunchback's claim, everyone thought it was a trumped-up business. And the town, knowing Miss Amelia, decided that surely she had put him out of the house after feeding him. But towards evening, when the sky had whitened, and the shift was done, a woman claimed to have seen a crooked face at the window of one of the rooms up over the store. Miss Amelia herself said nothing. She clerked in the store for a while, argued for an hour with a farmer over a plough shaft, mended some chicken wire, locked up near sundown, and went to her rooms. The town was left puzzled and talkative.

The next day Miss Amelia did not open the store, but stayed locked up inside her premises and saw no one. Now this was the day that the rumour started—the rumour so terrible that the town and all the country about were stunned by it. The rumour was started by a weaver called Merlie Ryan. He is a man of not much account—sallow, shambling, and with no teeth in his head. He has the three-day malaria, which means that every third day the fever comes on him. So on two days he is dull and cross, but on the third day he livens up and sometimes has an idea or two, most of which are foolish. It was while Merlie Ryan was in his fever that he turned suddenly and said:

'I know what Miss Amelia done. She murdered that man for something in that suitcase.'

He said this in a calm voice, as a statement of fact. And within an hour the news had swept through the town. It was a fierce and sickly tale the town built up that day. In it were all the things which cause the heart to shiver—a hunchback, a midnight burial in the swamp, the dragging of Miss Amelia through the streets of the town on the way to prison, the squabbles over what would happen to her property—all told in hushed voices and repeated with some fresh and weird detail. It rained and women forgot to bring in the washing from the lines. One or two mortals, who were in debt to Miss Amelia, even put on Sunday clothes as though it were a holiday. People clustered together on the main street, talking and watching the store.

It would be untrue to say that all the town took part in this evil festival. There were a few sensible men who reasoned that Miss Amelia, being rich, would not go out of her way to murder a vagabond for a few trifles of junk. In the town there were even three good people, and they did not want this crime, not even for sake of the interest and the great commotion it would entail; it gave them no pleasure to think of Miss Amelia holding to the bars of the penitentiary and being electrocuted in Atlanta. These good people judged Miss Amelia in a different way from what the others judged her. When a person is as contrary in every single respect as she was and when the sins of a person have amounted to such a point that they can hardly be remembered all at once—then this person plainly requires a special judgement. They remembered that Miss Amelia had been born dark and somewhat queer of face, raised motherless by her father who was a solitary man, that early in youth she had grown to be six feet two inches tall which in itself is not natural for a woman, and that her ways and habits of life were too peculiar ever to reason about. Above all, they remembered her puzzling marriage, which was the most unreasonable scandal ever to happen in this town.

So these good people felt towards her something near to pity. And when she was out on her wild business, such as rushing in a house to drag forth a sewing-machine in payment for a debt, or getting herself worked up over some matter concerning the law— they had towards her a feeling which was a mixture of exasperation, a ridiculous little inside tickle, and a deep, unnameable sadness. But enough of the good people, for there were only three of them; the rest of the town was making a holiday of this fancied crime the whole of the afternoon.

Miss Amelia herself, for some strange reason, seemed unaware of all this. She spent most of her day upstairs. When down in the store, she prowled around peacefully, her hands deep in the pockets of her overalls and her head bent so low that her chin was tucked inside the collar of her shirt. There was no bloodstain on her anywhere. Often she stopped and just stood sombrely looking down at the cracks in the floor, twisting a lock of her short-cropped hair, and whispering something to herself. But most of the day was spent upstairs.

Dark came on. The rain that afternoon had chilled the air, so that the evening was bleak and gloomy as in winter-time. There were no stars in the sky, and a light, icy drizzle had set in. The lamps in the houses made mournful, wavering flickers when watched from the street. A wind had come up, not from the swamp side of the town but from the cold black pinewoods to the north.

The clocks in the town struck eight. Still nothing had happened. The bleak night, after the gruesome talk of the day, put a fear in some people, and they stayed home close to the fire. Others were gathered in groups together. Some eight or ten men had convened on the porch of Miss Amelia's store. They were silent and were indeed just waiting about. They themselves did not know what they were waiting for, but it was this: in times of tension, when some great action is impending, men gather and wait in this way. And after a time there will come a moment when all together they will act in unison, not from thought or from the will of any one man, but as though their instincts had merged together so that the decision belongs to no single one of them, but to the group as a whole. At such a time no individual hesitates. And whether the joint action will result in ransacking, violence, and crime, depends on destiny. So the men waited soberly on the porch of Miss Amelia's store, not one of them realising what they would do, but knowing inwardly that they must wait, and that the time had almost come.

CARSON MCCULLERS

Questions

1 'By noon, of course, everyone had heard . . .' (l. 4). What does that 'of course' tell us about the neighbourhood?

2 'And the town, knowing Miss Amelia, decided that surely she had put him out of the house after feeding him' (l. 12). What does this tell us about Miss Amelia and her neighbours' attitude towards her?

3 *a* How reliable was Merlie Ryan?
 b Was there any evidence to support his accusation?
 c Did any facts contradict Merlie Ryan's statement?

4 Why did some people put on their Sunday clothes? Why does the author call it an 'evil festival' (l. 46)?

5 How many 'good people' were there in the town? How did they feel about Miss Amelia?

6 What did Miss Amelia do that might have aroused people's suspicions?

7 Find two examples of how these people felt that even the weather confirmed their suspicions.

8 Why did the men finally gather on Miss Amelia's porch? What were their intentions?

9 What possible lines of action were open to these waiting men?

10 Are there any reasons for thinking that most of her neighbours actually hoped that Miss Amelia had committed some terrible crime?

Implications

11 In what ways was Miss Amelia odd? How do people react to an odd person in a neighbourhood? Should such a person try to be like other people?

3

4

12 What difficulties might you encounter if you tried to help a lonely person?

13 These townsfolk were united by suspicion. What are the dangers, for any group of people, of unity at any cost?

14 Why did the people accept Merlie Ryan's statement on the murder? Why should people at any time actually want someone to have done something that they can condemn? Have you any experience of this yourself?

15 From your experiences of doing anything with a group of others, how true do you find the author's account of the men preparing to take action together?

Exercises

16 Imagine you are a reporter in the town you have just read about, sending news to your office by telegram. Write a series of five or six telegrams that you would have sent as the suspicions and events developed.

17 Give an account of a rumour that spread in your neighbourhood—how it was passed on, people's reactions, and what truth, if any, there was in it.

18 Make two lists of actions that people are most likely to carry out only when in a group, one list of actions that you approve of, one list of actions you disapprove of.

19 Write a paragraph describing someone you know who is odd or a misfit.

Discussion and Writing

Photograph No. 3 (facing page 34)

Are the two women talking, shopping, or is one of them selling to the other?

What time of day would you say it was?

Can you say anything else about the district?

Write about the people you meet if you are sent out shopping.

4 *Law and Order* (*Who shall rule?*)

¶ *How often in your day-to-day life do you have to do what someone else tells you? How often do you give orders to anyone else?*

¶ *Whom are you willing to take orders from? Whom do you obey but only unwillingly?*

¶ *Whom would you choose as a leader among your form mates and why?*

¶ *In this story a group of boys survive an air crash and are alone on a tropical island.*

Lord of the Flies

Ralph flung back his hair. One arm pointed at the empty horizon. His voice was loud and savage, and struck them into silence.

'There was a ship.'

Jack, faced at once with too many awful implications, ducked away from them. He laid a hand on the pig and drew his knife. Ralph brought his arm down, fist clenched, and his voice shook.

'There was a ship. Out there. You said you'd keep the fire going and you let it out!' He took a step towards Jack who turned and faced him.

'They might have seen us. We might have gone home——'

This was too bitter for Piggy, who forgot his timidity in the agony of his loss. He began to cry out, shrilly:

'You and your blood, Jack Merridew! You and your hunting! We might have gone home——'

Ralph pushed Piggy on one side.

'I was chief; and you were going to do what I said. You talk. But you can't even build huts—then you go off hunting and let out the fire——'

He turned away, silent for a moment. Then his voice came again on a peak of feeling.

'There was a ship——'

One of the smaller hunters began to wail. The dismal truth was filtering through to everybody. Jack went very red as he hacked and pulled at the pig.

'The job was too much. We needed everyone.'

Ralph turned.

'You could have had everyone when the shelters were finished. But you had to hunt——'

'We needed meat.'

Jack stood up as he said this, the bloodied knife in his hand. The two boys faced each other. There was the brilliant world of hunting, tactics, fierce exhilaration, skill; and there was the world of longing and baffled commonsense. Jack transferred the knife to his left hand and smudged blood over his forehead as he pushed down the plastered hair.

Piggy began again.

'You didn't ought to have let that fire out. You said you'd keep the smoke going——'

This from Piggy, and the wails of agreement from some of the hunters drove Jack to violence. The bolting look came into his blue eyes. He took a step, and able at last to hit someone, stuck his fist into Piggy's stomach. Piggy sat down with a grunt. Jack stood over him. His voice was vicious with humiliation.

'You would, would you? Fatty!'

Ralph made a step forward and Jack smacked Piggy's head. Piggy's glasses flew off and tinkled on the rocks. Piggy cried out in terror:

'My specs!'

He went crouching and feeling over the rocks but Simon, who got there first, found them for him. Passions beat about Simon on the mountain-top with awful wings.

'One side's broken.'

Piggy grabbed and put on the glasses. He looked malevolently at Jack.

'I got to have them specs. Now I only got one eye. Jus' you wait——'

Jack made a move towards Piggy who scrambled away till a great rock lay between them. He thrust his head over the top and glared at Jack through his one flashing glass.

'Now I only got one eye. Just you wait——'

Jack mimicked the whine and scramble.

'Jus' you wait—yah!'

Piggy and the parody were so funny that the hunters began to laugh. Jack felt encouraged. He went on scrambling and the laughter rose to a gale of hysteria. Unwillingly Ralph felt his lips twitch; he was angry with himself for giving way.

He muttered.

'That was a dirty trick.'

Jack broke out of his gyration and stood facing Ralph. His words came out in a shout.

'All right, all right!'

He looked at Piggy, at the hunters, at Ralph.

'I'm sorry. About the fire, I mean. There. I——'

He drew himself up.

'——I apologise.'

The buzz from the hunters was one of admiration at this handsome behaviour. Clearly they were of the opinion that Jack had done the decent thing, had put himself in the right by his generous apology and Ralph, obscurely, in the wrong. They waited for an appropriately decent answer.

Yet Ralph's throat refused to pass one. He resented, as an addition to Jack's misbehaviour, this verbal trick. The fire was dead, the ship was gone. Could they not see? Anger instead of decency passed his throat.

'That was a dirty trick.'

They were silent on the mountain-top while the opaque look appeared in Jack's eyes and passed away.

Ralph's final word was an ungracious mutter.

'All right. Light the fire.'

With some positive action before them, a little of the tension died. Ralph said no more, did nothing, stood looking down at the ashes round his feet. Jack was loud and active. He gave orders, sang, whistled, threw remarks at the silent Ralph, remarks that did not need an answer, and therefore could not invite a snub; and still Ralph was silent. No one, not even Jack, would ask him to move and in the end they had to build the fire three yards away and in a place not really as convenient. So Ralph asserted his chieftainship and could not have chosen a better way if he had thought for days. Against this weapon, so indefinable and so effective, Jack was powerless and raged without knowing why. By the time the pile was built, they were on different sides of a high barrier.

When they had dealt with the fire another crisis arose. Jack had no means of lighting it. Then to his surprise, Ralph went to Piggy and took the glasses from him. Not even Ralph knew how a link between him and Jack had been snapped and fastened elsewhere.

'I'll bring 'em back.'

'I'll come too.'

Piggy stood behind him, islanded in a sea of meaningless colour,

while Ralph knelt and focused the glossy spot. Instantly the fire was
110 alight Piggy held out his hands and grabbed the glasses back.

WILLIAM GOLDING

Questions

1 'The dismal truth was filtering through to everybody' (l. 22). What was this truth?

2 Is there anything to show that Jack feels in any way guilty about the fire?

3 Why were Piggy's specs so valuable?

4 Why does Jack poke fun at Piggy in his distress over his broken specs?

5 'Unwillingly Ralph felt his lips twitch; he was angry with himself for giving way' (l. 65). Why is Ralph angry with himself? How does he react as a result?

6 Why is Jack's apology popular with the hunters?

7 Why does Ralph resent this apology as a 'verbal trick' (l. 82)?

8 How does Ralph assert his chieftainship, and why could he 'not have chosen a better way if he had thought for days' (l. 98)?

9 'By the time the pile was built, they were on different sides of a high barrier' (l. 100). Explain the double meaning of this.

10 'Not even Ralph knew how a link between him and Jack had been snapped and fastened elsewhere' (l. 104). What was the link? Where had it been refastened?

Implications

11 How do the other boys respond to Ralph, Jack and Piggy?

12 How could you sum up the differences in outlook between Ralph and Jack?

13 Later in the story Ralph says to himself 'Piggy could think... only Piggy was no chief.' Is there any evidence, in this passage, of Piggy's common sense? Why should Ralph think Piggy was no chief?

14 What happens to a group of people who want to work together but cannot agree amongst themselves? Think in terms of a definite group such as—a camping party, a dance committee, a club.

15 Suppose such a group does reach agreement. What more is needed in order to get things done?

16 What is there in this extract to show that the boys depended on each other?

17 As far as you can tell in these circumstances, which boy would make the best leader?

Exercises

18 Draw up a set of about ten essential rules for a group of boys, like these, alone on a tropical island.

19 As if you were one of this group, write a letter of distress that you are going to seal into a bottle and throw into the sea.

¶ *Many young people in their first employment are sent away to another part of the country on training courses. If sent away from home, friends and relations like this, what would you miss most?*

¶ *How would you feel if you were one of a team on a distant away match and the leader of your party disappeared with the return tickets? What would you do? Who would be your spokesman?*

¶ *Imagine an army cut off without its leader, two thousand miles behind enemy lines. This actually happened as reported, over two thousand years ago.*

The Persian Expedition

The others went round the various detachments and where there was a general still alive they called for him, or, in cases where he was missing, for his deputy commander; where there was a captain still alive, they called for the captain. When they had all assembled they sat down in front of the place where the arms were kept. The generals and captains assembled there were about a hundred all together, and the meeting took place at about midnight. Hieronymus of Elis, the oldest of Proxenus's captains, then began the proceedings and spoke as follows: 'Generals and captains, in view of our present position we decided to meet together ourselves and to invite you to join us, so that, if possible, we might come to some useful decision. I now call upon Xenophon to speak as he has already spoken to us.'

Xenophon accordingly spoke as follows: 'Here is one thing which we all know, namely, that the King and Tissaphernes have made prisoners of all those of us whom they could and are obviously planning, if they can manage it, to destroy the rest of us. Our part, as I see it, is to do everything possible to prevent our ever coming into the power of the natives—indeed to see rather that they are in our power. I should like to assure you of this point—that you who have assembled here in your present numbers are placed in an extraordinarily responsible position. All these soldiers of ours have their eyes on you, and if they see that you are downhearted they will all become cowards, while if you are yourselves clearly prepared to meet the enemy and if you call on the rest to do their part, you can be sure that they will follow you and try to be like you. It is right, too, I think, that you should show some superiority over them. After all you are generals, you are officers and captains. In peace time you got more pay and more respect than they did. Now, in war time, you ought to hold yourselves to be braver than the general mass of men, and to take decisions for the rest, and, if necessary, to be the first to do the hard work. I think that first of all you could do a great service to the army by appointing generals and captains as quickly as possible to take the places of those whom we have lost. For where there is no one in control nothing useful or distinguished can ever get done. This is roughly true of all departments of life, and entirely true where soldiering is concerned. Here it is discipline that makes one feel safe, while lack of discipline has destroyed many people before now.

'Then I think that, after you have appointed the required number of officers, if you were to call a meeting of the rest of the soldiers and put some heart into them, that would be just what the occasion demands. At the moment I expect you realise, just as I do, how dispirited they were in handing in their arms for the night and in going on guard. In that condition I cannot see how any use can be made of them, whether by night or by day. But there will be a great rise in their spirits if one can change the way they think, so that instead of having in their heads the one idea of "what is going to happen to me?" they may think "what action am I going to take?"

'You are well aware that it is not numbers or strength that bring the victories in war. No, it is when one side goes against the enemy with the gods' gift of a stronger morale that their adversaries, as a rule, cannot withstand them. I have noticed this point too, my friends, that in soldiering the people whose one aim is to keep alive usually find a wretched and dishonourable death, while the people who, realising that death is the common lot of all men, make it their endeavour to die with honour, somehow seem more often to reach old age and to have a happier life when they are alive. These are facts which you too should realise (our situation demands it) and should show that you yourselves are brave men and should call on the rest to do likewise.'

So he ended his speech. Chirisophus spoke after him and said: 'Up to now, Xenophon, the only thing I knew about you was that I had heard you were an Athenian. Now I congratulate you on your speech and your actions, and I should like to see here as many people of your sort as possible. Then we should have the right spirit all through the army. And now,' he went on, 'let us not waste time, my friends. Let us go away, and let those who are short of officers choose new ones. When you have chosen them, come to the centre of the camp and bring along those whom you have elected. Then we will muster the rest of the soldiers there. Tolmides the herald had better come with us.'

XENOPHON
translated by REX WARNER

Questions

1 How does Hieronymus of Elis reassure the assembled officers that no one is taking over the leadership without their agreement?

2 When Xenophon speaks, he starts with a warning. What is this warning?

3 He goes on to remind the officers of their responsibility as leaders. What effect does he say their morale will have upon that of their men?

4 What three things does Xenophon say are expected of an officer in wartime?

5 Why does Xenophon think it is so urgent to replace all lost officers?

6 How does Xenophon know the men are dispirited, and what does he say will be the result of this?

7 What, according to Xenophon, is the greatest factor in the winning of battles?

8 Further to this, how does Xenophon compare the cowardly and the brave?

9 What were the officers going to do as soon as new officers had been appointed?

10 How did the Greeks appoint new officers?

Implications

11 In how many ways does Xenophon imply that the example set by leaders has its effect right down the ranks? Do you agree that everybody needs an example to follow?

12 'Where there is no one in control nothing useful or distinguished can ever get done' (l. 35). Xenophon says this is true of all walks of life, not only soldiering. Do you find this to be true, for example, in (*a*) the home, (*b*) an office, (*c*) a factory, (*d*) a team?

13 Why do you think Chirisophus congratulates Xenophon and shows readiness to serve under him?

14 If a person is voted into a position of authority, why should those who voted obey him? (Think first of actual examples like a team captain or any other group leader, or of local councillors who may approve of local by-laws.)

15 In many city states of Ancient Greece the whole adult male population would regularly meet and vote on matters of government. They called this 'democracy'. When and where today would such a method of action be possible, and at what level would it be impracticable?

Exercises

16 Sum up the argument of Xenophon's speech by writing down his main points in the order in which he makes them.

17 Suppose you were a Greek soldier preparing to travel a long distance expecting lots of sudden action. List the essential items you would carry.

18 Write a composition with the title 'How we stuck together', or 'Choosing a leader', or 'When I take orders and when I don't'.

19 Make a list of the things you would most miss if away from home and friends.

HOME AND ABOUT

¶ *Have you ever changed loyalty from one leader to another, say by leaving one gang, club, society for another? Why did you do so?*

¶ *If you wanted to change the leader of such a group, how would you go about it?*

The Death of Grass

[Imagine this country reduced to a state of complete chaos and anarchy by worldwide famine. Armed bands prowl the land in search of food. One band of six adults and four children, led by John Custance, is making for Blind Gill, a safe valley in Westmorland. They have only three guns between them, when they meet another band led by Joe Ashton.]

Pirrie said: 'Custance! Up the road, there.'

Between Baugh Fell and Rise Hill, the road ran straight for about three-quarters of a mile. There were figures on it, coming down towards them.

This was a large party—seven or eight men, with women and some children. They walked with confidence along the crown of the road, and even at that distance they were accompanied by what looked like the glint of guns.

John said with satisfaction: 'That's what we want.'

Roger said: 'If they'll talk. They may be the kind that shoot first. We could get over behind the wall before we try opening the conversation.'

'If we did, it might give them reason to shoot first.'

'The women and children, then.'

'Same thing. Their own are out in the open.'

Most of the men seemed to be carrying guns. John could eventually make out a couple of army pattern ·300 rifles, a Winchester ·202, and the inevitable shot-guns. With increasing assurance, he thought: this is it. This was enough to get them through any kind of chaos to Blind Gill. There only remained the problem of winning them over.

He had hoped they would halt a short distance away, but they had neither suspicion nor doubts of their own ability to meet any challenge, and they came on. Their leader was a burly man, with a heavy red face. He wore a leather belt, with a revolver stuck in it.

As he came abreast of where John's party stood by the side of the road, he glanced at them indifferently. It was another good sign that he did not covet their guns; or not enough, at least, even to contemplate fighting for them.

John called to him: 'Just a minute.'

He stopped and looked at John with a deliberation of movement that was impressive. His accent when he spoke was thickly Yorkshire.

'You wanted summat?'

'My name's John Custance. We're heading for a place I know, up in the hills. My brother's got land there—in a valley that's blocked at one end and only a few feet wide at the other. Once in there, you can keep an army out. Are you interested?'

He considered for a moment. 'What are you telling us for?'

John pointed down towards the valley. 'Things are nasty down there. Too nasty for a small party like ours. We're looking for recruits.'

The man grinned. 'Happen we're not looking for a change. We're doin' all right.'

'You're doing all right now,' John said, 'while there are potatoes in the ground, and meat to be looted from farmhouses. But it won't be too long before the meat's used up, and there won't be any to follow it. You won't find potatoes in the fields next year, either.'

'We'll look after that when the time comes.'

'I can tell you how. By cannibalism. Are you looking forward to it?'

The leader himself was still contemptuously hostile, but there was some response, John thought, in the ranks behind him. He could not have had long to weld his band together; there would be cross-currents, perhaps counter-currents.

The man said: 'Maybe we'll have the taste for it by then. I don't think as I could fancy you at the moment.'

'It's up to you,' John said. He looked past him to where the women and children were; there were five women, and four children, their ages varying between five and fifteen. 'Those who can't find a piece of land which they can hold are going to end up by being savages—if they survive at all. That may suit you. It doesn't suit us.'

'I'll tell you what doesn't suit me, mister—a lot of talk. I never had no time for gabbers.'

'You won't need to talk at all in a few years ' John said. 'You'll be back to grunts and sign language. I'm talking because I've got something to tell you, and if you've got any sense you will see it's to your advantage to listen.'

'Our advantage, eh? It wouldn't be yours you're thinking about?'

'I'd be a fool if it wasn't. But you stand to get more out of it. We want temporary help so that we can get to my brother's place. We're offering you a place where you can live in something like peace, and rear your children to be something better than wild animals.'

The man glanced round at his followers, as though sensing an effect that John's words were having on them. He said:

'Still talk. You think we're going to take you on, and find ourselves on a wild-goose chase up in the hills?'

'Have you got a better place to go to? Have you got anywhere to go to, for that matter? What harm can it possibly do you to come along with us and find out?'

He stared at John, still hostile but baffled. At last, he turned to his followers.

'What do you reckon of it?' he said to them.

Before anyone spoke, he must have read the answer in their expressions.

'Wouldn't do any harm to go and have a look,' a dark, thickset man said. There was a murmur of agreement. The red-faced man turned back to John.

'Right,' he said. 'You can show us the way to the valley of your brother's. We'll see what we think of it when we get there. Whereabouts is it, anyway?'

Unprepared to reveal the location of Blind Gill, or even to name it, John was getting ready an evasive answer, when Pirrie intervened. He said coolly:

'That's Mr Custance's business, not yours. He's in charge here. Do as he tells you, and you will be all right.'

John heard a gasp of dismay from Ann. He himself found it hard to see a justification for Pirrie's insolence, both of manner and content; it could only re-confirm the leader of the other group in his hostility. He thought of saying something to take the edge off the remark, but was stopped both by the realisation that he wouldn't be likely to mend the situation, and by the trust he had come to have in Pirrie's judgement. Pirrie, undoubtedly, knew what he was doing.

'It's like that, is it?' the man said. 'We're to do as Custance tells us? You can think again about that. I do the ordering for my lot, and, if you join up with us, the same goes for you.'

'You're a big man,' Pirrie observed speculatively, 'but what the situation needs is brains. And there, I imagine, you fall short.'

The red-faced man spoke with incongruous softness:

'I don't take anything from little bastards just because they're little. There aren't any policemen round the corner now. I make my own regulations; and one of them is that people round me keep their tongues civil.'

Finishing, he tapped the revolver in his belt, to emphasise his words. As he did so, Pirrie raised his rifle. The man, in earnest now, began to pull the revolver out. But the muzzle was still inside his belt when Pirrie fired. From that short range, the bullet lifted him and crashed him backwards on the road. Pirrie stood in silence, his rifle at the ready.

Some of the women screamed. John's eyes were on the men opposing him. He had restrained his impulse to raise his own shotgun, and was glad to see that Roger also had not moved. Some of the other men made tentative movements towards their guns, but the incident had occurred too quickly for them, and too surprisingly. One of them half lifted a rifle; unconcernedly, Pirrie moved to cover him, and he set it down again.

John said: 'It's a pity about that.' He glanced at Pirrie. 'But he should have known better than to try threatening someone with a gun if he wasn't sure he could fire first. Well, the offer's still open. Anyone who wants to join us and head for the valley is welcome.'

One of the women had knelt down by the side of the fallen man. She looked up.

'He's dead.'

John nodded slightly. He looked at the others.

'Have you made up your minds yet?'

The thickset man, who had spoken before, said:

'I reckon it were his own look-out. I'll come along, all right. My name's Parsons—Alf Parsons.'

Slowly, with an air almost ritualistic, Pirrie lowered his rifle. He went across to the body, and pulled the revolver out of the belt. He took it by the muzzle, and handed it to John. Then he turned back to address the others:

'My name is Pirrie, and this is Buckley, on my right. As I said, Mr Custance is in charge here. Those who wish to join up with our little party should come along and shake hands with Mr Custance, and identify themselves. All right?'

Alf Parsons was the first to comply, but the others lined up behind him. Here, more than ever, ritual was being laid down. It might come, in time, to a bending of the knee, but this formal hand-shake was as clear a sign as that would have been of the rendering of fealty.

JOHN CHRISTOPHER

Questions

1 What reason had the approaching band for walking with confidence? What further evidence is there of this confidence?

2 Why does John Custance refuse to take cover as Roger suggests? As it turns out, was he wise in his decision?

3 How much exactly does John tell the strangers about Blind Gill?

4 What does John ask of the other party, and how does he make the suggestion seem reasonable?

5 How are these bands managing at this time for food supplies? What does John foresee will happen before long over food supplies?

6 What does John mean by 'You won't need to talk at all in a few years. You'll be back to grunts and sign language' (l. 65)?

7 Why is Joe Ashton 'baffled' (l. 81)?

8 Why were John and Ann (his wife) astonished at Pirrie's challenging remark 'Do as he tells you, and you will be all right' (l. 96)?

9 Why did John and Roger not raise their guns after Pirrie fired?

10 Why does Pirrie hand Ashton's revolver to John?

Implications

11 Why did John not disclose the name and position of Blind Gill?

12 To whose advantage would be John's suggestion of joining forces?

13 What did Joe Ashton dislike about John Custance? Is there anything to suggest that he also feared him?

14 Why do you think Pirrie supported John as his leader? What was the relationship between the two men?

15 In the situation described, who do you think was most fitted to lead the others, and why?

16 Can you explain the use of the words 'ritual' and 'ritualistic' at the end of the passage?

17   Is it necessary to have leaders at all, (*a*) in emergency situations, (*b*) in normal conditions?

Exercises

18   Give an eye-witness account of this scene as if you were (*a*) Pirrie, or (*b*) Roger, or (*c*) Alf Parsons.

19 *a*   Imagine you are Pirrie and write down your reasons for following John Custance as leader.
b   Imagine you are Alf Parsons and write down your reasons for first following Joe Ashton and then John Custance.

20   Think of someone you have followed as a leader. Make a list of his good points and bad points as a leader.

21   Describe an occasion when you yourself have seen two people competing for leadership, for instance within the family, in a gang, in a club election, in a sports team.

Discussion and Writing

Photograph No. 4 (facing page 35)

Speakers' Corner, Hyde Park. What has drawn people to listen here?

What can you tell of this speaker?

Should he be allowed to say anything he likes? What limits would you place on him? Would you accept that they should apply to you as well?

Compose this speaker's speech for him.

As for a debate, state the case for complete freedom of speech *or* the case for limitations on speech.

Two: Work and Leisure

5 Jobs

¶ *In the job of work you hope to do what sort of promotion would you look for? Why are some people never promoted?*

¶ *Do you think a young person at work should be given opportunity by his or her employer for further training? Should such training be compulsory?*

¶ *What could most easily make you hate the work you do?*

¶ *Should an employer be compelled to show good reason before dismissing an employee?*

Kipps

His round began at half-past six in the morning, when he would descend, unwashed and shirtless, in old clothes and a scarf, and dust boxes and yawn, and take down wrappers and clean the windows until eight. Then in half an hour he would complete his toilet, and take an austere breakfast of bread and margarine and what only an Imperial Englishman would admit to be coffee, after which refreshment he ascended to the shop for the labours of the day.

And now he had to stand by to furnish any help that was necessary to the seniors who served, to carry parcels and bills about the shop, to clear away 'stuff' after each engagement, to hold up curtains until his arms ached, and, what was more difficult than all, to do nothing and not stare disconcertingly at customers when there was nothing for him to do. He plumbed an abyss of boredom, or stood a mere carcass with his mind far away, fighting the enemies of the empire, or steering a dream-ship perilously into unknown seas. To be recalled sharply to our higher civilisation by some bustling senior's 'Nar then, Kipps. Look alive! Ketch 'old. (My Heart and Liver!)'

At half-past seven o'clock—except on late nights—a feverish activity of 'straightening up' began, and when the last shutter was up outside, Kipps, with the speed of an arrow leaving a bow, would start hanging wrappers over the fixtures and over the piles of wares upon the counters, preparatory to a vigorous scattering of wet sawdust and the sweeping out of the shop.

Sometimes people would stay long after the shop was closed. 'They don't mind a bit at Shalford's,' these ladies used to say, and while they loitered it was forbidden to touch a wrapper or take any measures to conclude the day until the doors closed behind them.

Mr Kipps would watch these later customers from the shadow of a stack of goods, and death and disfigurement was the least he wished for them. Rarely much later than nine, a supper of bread and cheese and watered beer awaited him downstairs, and, that consumed, the rest of the day was entirely at his disposal for reading, recreation, and the improvement of his mind. . . .

The front door was locked at half-past ten, and the gas in the dormitory extinguished at eleven.

On Sundays he was obliged to go to church once, and commonly he went twice, for there was nothing else to do. He sat in the free seats at the back; he was too shy to sing, and not always clever enough to keep his place in the Prayer Book, and he rarely listened to the sermon. But he had developed a sort of idea that going to church had a tendency to alleviate life. His aunt wanted to have him confirmed, but he evaded this ceremony for some years.

In the intervals between services he walked about Folkestone with an air of looking for something. Folkestone was not so interesting on Sundays as on week-days because the shops were shut; but, on the other hand, there was a sort of confusing brilliance along the front of the Leas in the afternoon. Sometimes the apprentice next above him would condescend to go with him; but when the apprentice next but one above him condescended to go with the apprentice next above him, then Kipps, being habited as yet in ready-made clothes without tails, and unsuitable, therefore, to appear in such company, went alone.

At times there came breaks in this routine—sale-times, darkened by extra toil and work past midnight, but brightened by a sprat supper and some shillings in the way of 'premiums'. And every year—not now and then, but every year—Mr Shalford, with parenthetic admiration of his own generosity and glancing comparisons with the austerer days when he was apprenticed, conceded Kipps no less than ten days holiday—ten whole days every year! Many a poor soul at Portland might well envy the fortunate Kipps. Insatiable heart of man! but how those days were grudged and counted as they snatched themselves away from him one after another!

Once a year came stocktaking, and at intervals gusts of 'marking off' goods newly arrived. Then the splendours of Mr Shalford's being shone with oppressive brilliancy. 'System!' he would say, 'system! Come! 'ussell' and issue sharp, confusing, contradictory orders very quickly.

A vague self-disgust that shaped itself as an intense hate of Shalford and all his fellow-creatures filled the soul of Kipps during these periods of storm and stress. He felt that the whole business was unjust and idiotic, but the why and the wherefore was too much for his unfortunate brain. His mind was a welter. One desire, the desire to dodge some, at least, of a pelting storm of disagreeable comment, guided him through a fumbling performance of his duties. His disgust was infinite! It was not decreased by the inflamed ankles and sore feet that form a normal incident in the business of making an English draper, and the senior apprentice Minton, a gaunt, sullen-faced youngster with close-cropped, wiry, black hair, a loose, ugly mouth, and a moustache like a smudge of ink, directed his attention to deeper aspects of the question and sealed his misery.

'When you get too old to work they chuck you away,' said Minton. 'Lor! you find old drapers everywhere—tramps, beggars, dock labourers, bus conductors—Quod. Anywhere but in a crib.'

'Don't they get shops of their own?'

'Lord! 'Ow are they to get shops of their own? They 'aven't any Capital! How's a draper's shopman to save up five hundred pounds even? I tell you it can't be done. You got to stick to Cribbs until it's over. I tell you we're in a blessed drain-pipe, and we've got to crawl along it till we die.'

H. G. WELLS

Questions

1 How did Kipps try to overcome his boredom in the shop?

2 Why did Kipps wish 'death and disfigurement' to late shoppers?

3 What evidence is there to show that the apprentices were kept as cheaply as possible?

4 What two reasons had Kipps for going to church?

5 Why was Kipps unlikely to make close friends with any of the other apprentices?

6 Why did Mr Shalford think that the holidays he allowed his apprentices were very generous?

7 How can we tell that Mr Shalford was not as efficient and systematic as he made out?

8 What future had Kipps obviously expected for a well-trained draper?

9 Why, according to Minton, was a draper's assistant unlikely ever to rise any higher?

10 Why did Kipps hate Shalford even before Minton's gloomy account of their prospects?

Implications

11 Which is more wearing—hard work or boredom?

12 Comment on H. G. Wells's sarcasm in 'the rest of the day was entirely at his disposal' (l. 34).

13 Discuss the value of the training that Kipps was getting from Shalford. What was he learning about drapery?

14 What should be the purpose of apprenticeship or trainee schemes? What rights should an apprentice or trainee have?

15 Which is more important—starting wage or prospects of promotion? How would you balance them?

16 Not everyone can rise far in a job or profession. What is the least that a reliable employee should be able to look forward to if not to crawl along a drainpipe till he dies?

Exercises

17 Put yourself in Mr Shalford's position and draw up a set of rules for his apprentices.

18 Imagine Mr Shalford addressing his staff on the subject of annual holidays. Write his speech.

19 Put yourself in Arthur Kipps's place and write a letter home about life at Mr Shalford's.

20 Make a list of questions that you would want to ask a possible employer before taking up a job with him.

¶ What is the difference between skill and hard labour?

¶ What is meant by 'craftsmanship', and what degree of craftsmanship will you need in the job you hope to take up?

¶ How much of this craftsmanship will you have picked up before leaving school? How much more, and from whom, do you hope to learn?

The Wheelwright's Shop

[Here is a wheelwright telling of the craftsman's work on the stock, or hub, of a cartwheel.]

Of the stock (the nave or hub) I hardly dare speak, such a fine product it was, and so ignorant about it do I feel. It is true I learnt to buy stocks with confidence in my own judgement; I seasoned them, chopped them into shape, chose them at last even to satisfy Cook. Nay, he occasionally asked my opinion, if anything dubious was discovered in working. But, as I had never enough skill of hand and eye myself, I always entrusted the actual turning and mortising of stocks to a trusty man—(Cook as long as he lived, and after him preferably Hole). These men, I knew, would sooner have been discharged than work badly, against their own conscience. So I left the stocks to them, only liking to look at each stock when it was brought from the lathe, and to 'weight' it (poise it) in my arms and hear the wheelwright say 'rare stock that'. His enthusiasm was catching. I felt a glow of pride in having ministered, however humbly, to so noble a tradition. Then I left the stock again to the workman.

A lumpish cylinder in shape—eleven or twelve inches in diameter and twelve or thirteen inches from end to end—a newly turned stock was a lovely thing—to the eyes, I thought, but more truly to sentiment, for the associations it hinted at. Elm from hedgerow or park, it spoke of open country. Well seasoned, it was a product of winter labour, of summer care in my own loft under my own hands. Long quiet afternoons it had lain there, where I could glance from the stocks across the town to the fields and the wooded hills. I had turned it over and over, had chopped the bark away, had brushed off the mildew while the quiet winter darkness had stolen through the shed, and at last I had chosen the stock for use, and put it into Cook's hands.

And now it lay, butter-coloured, smooth, slightly fragrant, soon to begin years of field-work, after much more skill—the skill of ancient England—had been bestowed on it, though already telling of that skill in every curve. Certainly we did not consciously remember all these matters at the time: rather we concerned ourselves with the utility this block of elm would have, with its grip for many years of the oak spokes to be driven into it by and by. But without thinking, we felt the glamour of the strong associations; and the skilled craftsmen must have felt it more than I, because they lived in that glamour as fishes live in water. They knew, better than any other may do, the answer of the elm when the keen blade goes searching between its molecules. This was, this is, for ever out of my reach. Only, I used to get some fellow-feeling about it, looking at a newly turned stock. I understood its parts—the shallow hollows at back and front where the blacksmith would presently put on the bonds, the sloping 'nose', the clean chisel-cut of the 'breast stroke'. This last was cut in all round the stock to mark where the face of the spokes was to be.

So, when I had had my look, the wheel-maker—Cook or another —carried the stock to his bench, there to mark on it with straddling compasses the place for the first auger-holes, preliminary to mortising it for the spokes. A tricky job, this. One young man, I remember, marking out his stock, prepared for an odd number of spokes—eleven or thirteen; though, every felloe (sections of the wheel's rim) requiring two, the spokes were always in even numbers; which error he did not detect until he had bored his stock and spoilt it. Too big for the fire, and too cross-grained to be easily split and thrown away, it lay about for months, an eyesore to the luckless youth who had spoilt it and a plain indication that it is not quite easy to mark a stock correctly.

Likewise was it not altogether a simple thing, though the skilled man seemed to find it easy enough, to fix the wobbly stock down for working upon. It was laid across a 'wheel-pit'—a narrow trench with sills, about three feet deep—where iron clamps, themselves tightly wedged into the sills, held the stock steady back and front. Then the mortices were started, with auger-holes. How easy it looked! In my childhood I had heard the keen auger biting into the elm, had delighted in the springy spiral borings taken out; but now I learnt that only a strong and able man could make them.

GEORGE STURT

Questions

1 What is meant by 'seasoning' (l. 3) timber? What tasks connected with it does George Sturt mention?

2 Why did Sturt not 'turn and mortise' (l. 7) the stocks himself?

3 Point out two pieces of evidence of Sturt's high respect for his craftsmen.

4 Two types of wood are mentioned. What was the use of each in the construction of a wheel?

5 How do we know, from what George Sturt writes, that these wheelwrights used experience passed down in a long tradition?

6 What other craftsman is mentioned as having a part to play in the construction of a wheel?

7 Why should a wheel always have had an even number of spokes?

8 Why was the ruined stock left lying about? What resulted from this?

9 What is there to show that George Sturt had grown up among wheelwrights and their work?

10 How can we tell that, although he was familiar with the craft, Sturt started to practise it too late in life to become skilled in it?

Implications

11 'How easy it looked.' How is it that a skilled worker can make his or her job look easy? Give an example of work like this that you have watched. Did you try it yourself?

12 Why do you think George Sturt's men 'would sooner have been discharged than work badly' (l. 9)?

13 How far is the design of an object (i.e. the shape it is to take) determined by the use to which it will be put? Is it possible for a product to be fully practical and at the same time satisfying to look at and to handle? You will need to think of actual examples and, if possible, collect them, or illustrations of them, for discussion.

14 If you are going to make something to your own design, what would you consider first in choosing (*a*) your material, (*b*) its shaping?

WORK AND LEISURE

15 What examples can you see around you of good craftsmanship and bad?

16 In which jobs open to you will good craftsmanship still count? What length of training would you need before being proficient?

17 George Sturt could follow his material from the growing tree to the finished cart. Where is it possible today to follow a job through all its stages? In what jobs today can a workman see the results of his own contribution in a finished product?

18 What advantages over the old crafts have modern methods of mass production?

Exercises

19 Describe the making of any piece of work that you have designed yourself. Say why you made it, how you decided on its shape, and the stages of its construction.

20 Describe how you spoiled a piece of craft work. Did you have to abandon the whole job or only a part? Did you learn anything from the mistake?

21 Describe the work of any skilled craftsman whom you have watched.

22 Write a letter to a manufacturer complaining about a product that was badly made. Think of and use in your letter an article that you have actually found faulty.

23 *a* How many words or expressions with a special meaning for the wheelwright does George Sturt use? Make a list of these and their meanings.
b Make a similar list of technical terms used in any one other branch of skilled work (e.g. bricklaying, cabinet-making, fruit growing).

[*Note.* There is a fully reconstructed wheelwright's shop in the basement of the Science Museum.]

JOBS

¶ What would you feel about working alongside somebody who was doing poorer work than you and getting the same pay?

¶ Have you ever voluntarily carried on past the end of school time to finish off a job? Can you remember why you wanted to?

¶ Which would you rather do on a practical subject—two hours' continuous work, or three periods of forty minutes on different days? What are your reasons?

One Day in the Life of Ivan Denisovich

[This is an account of a group of convicts at work in one of Stalin's labour camps.]

And now Shukhov was no longer seeing that distant view where sun gleamed on snow. He was no longer seeing the prisoners as they wandered from the warming-up places all over the site, some to hack away at the pits they hadn't finished that morning, some to fix the mesh reinforcement, some to erect trusses in the workshops. Shukhov was seeing only his wall—from the junction where the blocks rose in steps, higher than his waist, to where it met Kilgas's. His thoughts and his eyes were feeling their way under the ice to the wall itself, the outer façade of the power-station, two blocks thick.
10   At the spot he was working on, the wall had previously been laid by some mason who was either incompetent or had scamped the job. But now Shukhov tackled the wall as if it was his own handiwork. There, he saw, was a cavity that couldn't be levelled up in one row: he'd have to do it in three, adding a little more mortar each time. And here the outer wall bellied a bit—it would take two rows to straighten that. He divided the wall mentally into the place where he would lay blocks, starting at the point where they rose in steps, and the place where Senka was working, on the right, up to Kilgas's section. There in the corner, he reckoned, Kilgas wouldn't hold
20   back, he would lay a few blocks for Senka, to make things easier for him. And, while they were pottering about in the corner, Shukhov would forge ahead and have half the wall built, so that this pair wouldn't be behindhand. He noted how many blocks he'd require for each of the places. And the moment the carriers brought the blocks up he shouted at Alyosha:
'Bring 'em to me. Put 'em here. And here.'

The barrows came up two at a time—one for Kilgas's wall, one for Shukhov's. The mortar steamed in the frost but held no real warmth in it. You slapped it on the wall with your trowel and if you dawdled it would freeze: and then you'd have to hit it with the side of a hammer—you couldn't scrape it off with a trowel. And if you laid a block a bit out of true, it would immediately freeze too and set crooked: then you'd have the back of your axe to knock it off and chip away the mortar.

But Shukhov made no mistakes. The blocks varied. If any had chipped corners or broken edges or lumps on their sides, he noticed it at once and saw which way up to lay them and where they would fit best on the wall.

Here was one. Shukhov took up some of the steaming mortar on his trowel and chucked it into the appropriate place, with his mind on the joint below (this would have to be just at the middle of the block he was going to lay). He chucked on just enough mortar to go under the one block. Then he snatched it from the pile—carefully though, so as not to tear his mittens, for with blocks you can do that in no time. He smoothed the mortar with his trowel and then —down with the block! And without losing a moment he levelled it, patting it with the side of the trowel—it wasn't lying quite trim—so that the wall should be truly in line and the block lie level both lengthwise and across. The mortar was already freezing.

Now if some mortar had oozed out to the side, you had to chop it off as quickly as possible with the edge of your trowel and fling it over the wall (in summer it would go under the next brick, but now that was impossible). Next you took another look at the joint below, for there were times when the block had partially crumbled. In that event, you slapped in some extra mortar where the defect was, and you didn't lay the block flat—you slid it from side to side, squeezing out the extra mortar between it and its neighbour. An eye on the plumb. An eye on the surface. Set. Next.

The work went with a swing. Once two rows were laid and the old faults levelled up it would go quite smoothly. But now was the time to keep your eyes skinned.

Shukhov forged ahead; he pressed along the outside wall to meet Senka. Senka had parted with Tiurin in the corner and was now working along the wall to meet him.

Shukhov winked at the mortar-carriers. Bring it up, bring it up. Steady now. Smart's the word. He was working so fast he hadn't time to wipe his nose.

He and Senka met and began to scoop out of the same mortar-hod. It didn't take them long to scrape it to the bottom.

'Mortar!' Shukhov shouted over the wall.

'Coming up!' shouted Pavlo.

Another load arrived. They emptied that one too—all the liquid mortar in it, anyhow. The rest had already frozen to the sides. Scrape it off yourselves! If you don't it's you who'll be taking it up and down again. Off you go! Next!

'Pavlo's asking how you're getting on for mortar,' someone called from below.

'Mix some more.'

'We've got half a box mixed.'

'Mix another.'

What a pace they set! They were driving along the fifth row now. They'd had to double themselves up when they were working on the first row, but now the wall had risen shoulder-high. And why shouldn't they race on?—there were no windows or doors to allow for, just a couple of adjoining blank walls and plenty of blocks. Shukhov should have stretched a string higher but there was no time for it.

'The eighty-second have gone off to hand in their tools,' Gopchik reported.

Tiurin looked at him witheringly.

'Mind your own business, you shrimp. Bring some blocks.'

Shukhov looked about. Yes, the sun was beginning to set. It had a greyish appearance as it sank in a red haze. And they'd got into the swing—couldn't be better. They'd started on the fifth row now. Ought to finish it today. Level it off.

The mortar-carriers were snorting like winded horses. Buinovsky was quite grey in the face. He might not be forty but he wasn't far off it.

The cold was growing keener. Busy as were Shukhov's hands, the frost nipped his fingers through the shabby mittens. And it was piercing his left boot too. He stamped his foot. Thud, thud.

By now he needn't stoop to the wall, but he still had to bend his aching back for each block and each scoop of mortar.

The rail clanged. The signal went dinning all over the site and reached the power-station. They'd been caught with some unused mortar. Eh, just when they'd got into the swing of it!

'Mortar! Mortar!' Tiurin shouted.

A new boxful had only just been mixed. They had to go on laying, there was no other way. If they left anything in the box, next morning they could throw the whole lot of it to hell—the mortar would have petrified, it wouldn't yield to a pickaxe.

'Don't let me down, brothers,' Shukhov shouted.

Kilgas was fuming. He didn't like speed-ups. But he pressed on all the same. What else could he do?

Pavlo ran up with a barrow, a trowel in his belt, and began laying himself. Five trowels on the job now.

Now look out for where the rows meet. Shukhov visualised what shape of block was needed there, and shoving a hammer into Alyosha's hand egged him on:

'Knock a bit off this one.'

Hasty work is scamped work. Now that all of them were racing one another Shukhov bided his time, keeping an eye on the wall. He pushed Senka to the left and took over the laying himself towards the main corner on the right. It would be a disaster if the walls overlapped or if the corner shouldn't be level. Cost them half a day's work tomorrow.

'Stop!' He shoved Pavlo away from a block and levelled it himself. And from his place in the corner he noticed that Senka's section was sagging. He hurried over to Senka and levelled it out with two blocks.

Everyone dashed to his job. They took Shukhov's hammer from him and wound up his string. The mortar-carriers and the blocklifters hurried down into the mortar-shop. They'd nothing more to do up there. Three masons remained on top, Kilgas, Senka, and Shukhov. Tiurin walked about to see how much wall they'd built. He was pleased. 'Not bad, eh? In half a day.'

ALEXANDER SOLZHENITSYN

Questions

1 What is Shukhov's opinion of the workmanship of the previous mason? On what does he base his opinion?

2 What effects did the intense cold have upon (*a*) the materials, and (*b*) the method of work?

3 What mistakes was Shukhov careful to avoid? What sort of mistakes could he see had already been made?

4 What are the prisoners building?

5 How did the kind of building that it was simplify the masons' work?

JOBS

6 Why was Tiurin so short-tempered towards Gopchik?

7 Why did the masons want to go on working after the signal to stop?

8 Why did Shukhov keep a particular watch on the work when there were five masons working on it?

9 What would be the consequences for the prisoners of badly finished work?

10 Why were the masons left all alone on their job?

Implications

11 How can we tell from the opening line that Shukhov was fully absorbed in his work?

12 Which details indicate that Shukhov was a skilled worker?

13 Should a worker be paid for the time spent on a job, or on the quality of his or her work?

14 Should convicts be put to work? If so, what sort of work?

15 How can anyone take pride in their work even when it is compulsory?

16 Is it fair to say that a good workman works well under any conditions and that therefore these conditions do not matter?

Exercises

17 Describe the most tiring job of work you have ever carried out.

18 List the tools and materials used on this job by Shukhov.

19 'Hasty work is scamped work', says Shukhov to himself (l. 121). Write about an occasion when you have seen the truth of this brought home.

Discussion and Writing

Photograph No. 5 (facing page 66)

What is this worker doing? How long do you think he has been at work?

What drawbacks might there be to his work? What advantages, compared to some other jobs?

Write down what he might be thinking.

6 Leisure

¶ *Should facilities for recreation be provided by local authorities? What do you find to do in your home district other than join in what someone else has organised?*

¶ *What do you consider is the ugliest feature of your home district, and what the most beautiful?*

Nottingham and the Mining Country

Now the colliers had also an instinct of beauty. The colliers' wives had not. The colliers were deeply alive, instinctively. But they had no daytime ambition, and no daytime intellect. They avoided, really, the rational aspect of life. They preferred to take life instinctively and intuitively. They didn't even care very profoundly about wages. It was the women, naturally, who nagged on this score. There was a big discrepancy, when I was a boy, between the collier who saw, at the best, only a brief few hours of daylight—often no daylight at all during the winter weeks—and the collier's wife, who had all the day to herself when the man was down pit.

The great fallacy is, to pity the man. He didn't dream of pitying himself, till agitators and sentimentalists taught him to. He was happy: or more than happy, he was fulfilled. Or he was fulfilled on the receptive side, not on the expressive. The collier went to the pub and drank in order to continue his intimacy with his mates. They talked endlessly, but it was rather of wonders and marvels, even in politics, than of facts. It was hard facts, in the shape of wife, money, and nagging home necessities, which they fled away from, out of the house to the pub, and out of the house to the pit.

The collier fled out of the house as soon as he could, away from the nagging materialism of the woman. With the women it was always: This is broken, now you've got to mend it! or else: We want this, that, and the other, and where is the money coming from? The collier didn't know and didn't care very deeply—his life was otherwise. So he escaped. He roved the countryside with his dog, prowling for a rabbit, for nests, for mushrooms, anything. He loved the countryside, just the indiscriminating feel of it. Or he loved just to sit on his heels and watch—anything or nothing. He was not intellectually interested. Life for him did not consist in facts, but in a flow. Very often, he loved his garden. And very often he had a genuine love of the beauty of flowers. I have known it often and often, in colliers.

Now the love of flowers is a very misleading thing. Most women love flowers as possessions, and as trimmings. They can't look at a flower, and wonder a moment, and pass on. If they see a flower that arrests their attention, they must at once pick it, pluck it. Possession! A possession! Something added on to me! And most of the so-called love of flowers to-day is merely this reaching out of possession and egoism: something I've got: something that embellishes me. Yet I've seen many a collier stand in his back garden looking down at a flower with that odd, remote sort of contemplation which shows a real awareness of the presence of beauty. It would not even be admiration, or joy, or delight, or any of those things which so often have a root in the possessive instinct. It would be a sort of contemplation: which shows the incipient artist.

The real tragedy of England, as I see it, is the tragedy of ugliness. The country is so lovely: the man-made England is so vile. I know that the ordinary collier, when I was a boy, had a peculiar sense of beauty, coming from his intuitive and instinctive consciousness, which was awakened down pit. And the fact that he met with just cold ugliness and raw materialism when he came up into daylight, and particularly when he came to the Square or the Breach, and to his own table, killed something in him, and in a sense spoiled him as a man.

Now though perhaps nobody knew it, it was ugliness which betrayed the spirit of man, in the nineteenth century. The great crime which the moneyed classes and promoters of industry committed in the palmy Victorian days was the condemning of the workers to ugliness, ugliness, ugliness: meanness and formless and ugly surroundings, ugly ideals, ugly religion, ugly hope, ugly love, ugly clothes, ugly furniture, ugly houses, ugly relationship between workers and employers. The human soul needs actual beauty even more than bread. The middle classes jeer at the colliers for buying pianos—but what is the piano, often as not, but a blind reaching out for beauty? To the woman it is a possession and a piece of furniture and something to feel superior about. But see the elderly colliers trying to learn to play, see them listening with queer alert faces to their daughter's execution of 'The Maiden's Prayer', and you will see a blind, unsatisfied craving for beauty. It is far more deep in the men than in the women. The women want show. The men want beauty, and still want it.

D. H. LAWRENCE

Questions

1 'They had no daytime ambition, and no daytime intellect' (l. 2). What makes Lawrence say this about the colliers?

2 What two reasons had the colliers for going to the pubs?

3 What do you think Lawrence means when he says that the colliers loved the 'indiscriminating feel' (l. 27) of the countryside?

4 Lawrence claims that colliers had 'an instinct of beauty' (l. 1). What examples does he give of this instinctive appreciation?

5 Why did the collier not care much about wages?

6 'The love of flowers is a very misleading thing' (l. 33). Explain the difference between the two ways of loving flowers that Lawrence mentions.

7 According to Lawrence, what had been the Victorian industrialists' greatest crime against the working class?

8 How and why does Lawrence defend the colliers who buy pianos?

9 Why does he not defend the wife's pride in her piano?

Implications

10 Is it fair to say, as Lawrence does, that 'The country is so lovely: the man-made England is so vile' (l. 47)?

11 'This is broken, now you've got to mend it!' Lawrence's colliers obviously detested jobs about the home. Why do so many people nowadays find satisfaction in carrying out their own household repairs, decorations and improvements?

12 Since 1929 when Lawrence wrote this, Television has replaced the pianos in many homes. Can it satisfy the same needs?

13 'The human soul needs actual beauty even more than bread' (l. 62). Do you agree? What better chances, if any, have people today of seeing and enjoying beauty?

Exercises

14 Write a letter to your local council complaining about the ugliest spot in the district, suggesting improvements.

15 Describe something you very much enjoy looking at and would miss if it were damaged or destroyed.

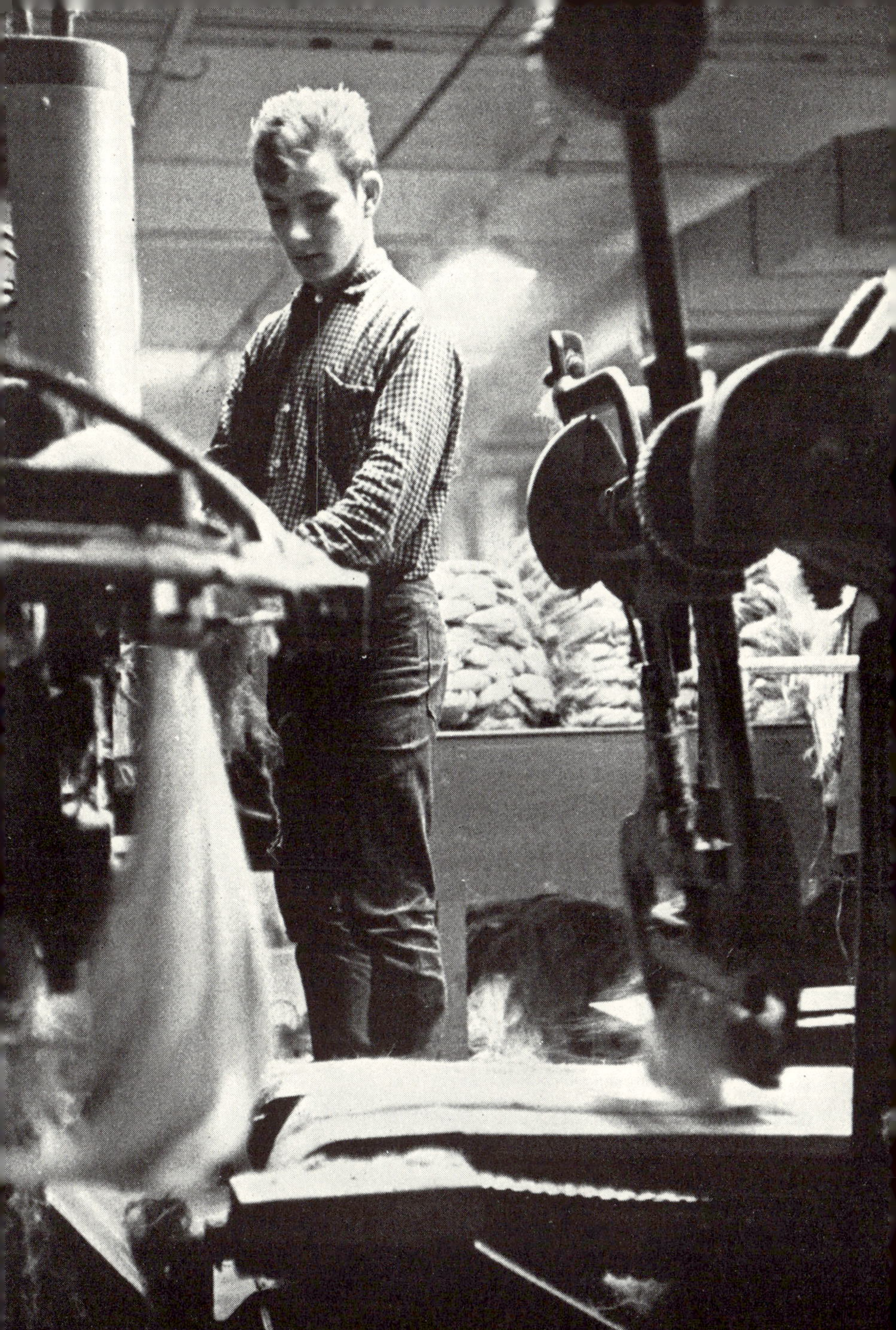

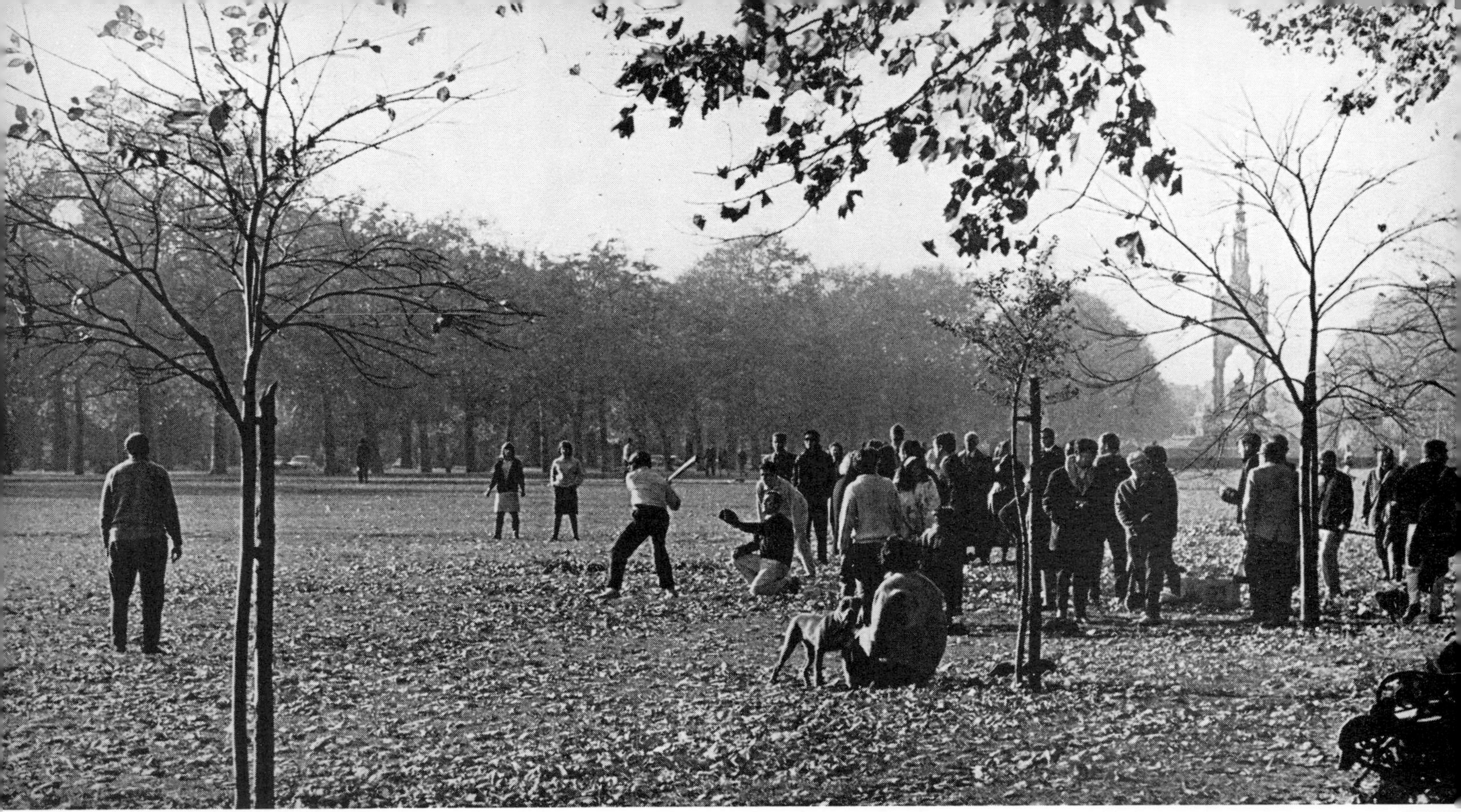

6

16 Make the necessary notes for a speech in defence of either the town or the country. Do not write out the speech; list the headings.

17 List the five most enjoyable ways you find of spending time in your own home and its immediate surroundings.

¶ *Is sport something to do, or something to watch?*

¶ *Who should be responsible for compensating a professional sportsman if he is injured?*

¶ *Should we pay other people to risk life and limb for our entertainment?*

The Ballad of Billy Rose

Outside Bristol Rovers Football Ground—
The date has gone from me, but not the day,
Nor how the dissenting flags in stiff array
Struck bravely out against the sky's grey round—

Near the Car Park then, past Austin and Ford,
Lagonda, Bentley, and a colourful patch
Of country coaches come in for the match
Was where I walked, having travelled the road

From Fishponds to watch Portsmouth in the Cup.
10 The Third Round, I believe. And I was filled
With the old excitement which had thrilled
Me so completely when, while growing up,

I went on Saturdays to match or fight.
Not only me; for thousands of us there
Strode forward eagerly, each man aware
Of vigorous memory, anticipating delight.

We all moved forward, all, except one man.
I saw him because he was paradoxically still,
A stone against the flood, face upright against us all,
20 Head bare, hoarse voice aloft. Blind as a stone.

WORK AND LEISURE

I knew him at once despite his pathetic clothes—
Something in his stance, or his sturdy frame
Perhaps. I could even remember his name
Before I saw it on his blind-man's tray. Billy Rose.

And twenty forgetful years fell away at the sight.
Bare-kneed, dismayed, memory fled to the hub
Of Saturday violence, with friends to the Labour Club,
Watching the boxing on a sawdust summer night.

The boys' enclosure close to the shabby ring
30　Was where we stood, clenched in a resin world,
Spoke in cool voices, lounged, were artificially bored
During minor bouts. We paid threepence to go in.

Billy Rose fought there. He was top of the bill.
So brisk a fighter, so gallant, so precise!
Trim as a tree he stood for the ceremonies,
Then turned to meet George Morgan of Triphil.

He had no chance. Courage was not enough,
Nor tight defence. Donald Davies was sick
And we threatened his cowardice with an embarrassed kick.
40　Ripped across both his eyes was Rose, but we were tough

And clapped him as they wrapped his blindness up
In busy towels, applauded the wave
He gave his executioners, cheered the brave
Blind man as he cleared with a jaunty hop

The top rope. I had forgotten that day
As if it were dead for ever, yet now I saw
Again the flowers of blood on the ring floor
As bright as his name. I cannot say

How long I stood with ghosts of the wild fists
50　And the cries of shaken boys long dead around me,
For struck to act at last, in terror and pity
I threw some frantic money, three treacherous pence—

And I cry at the memory—into his tray, and ran,
Entering the waves of the stadium like a drowning man.
Poor Billy Rose. God, he could fight
Before my three sharp coins knocked out his sight.

LESLIE NORRIS

Questions

1 How can we tell that the writer has been a lifelong sports fan?
2 What made Billy Rose stand out in the crowd outside the football stadium?
3 What was Billy Rose doing in this crowd?
4 What does Leslie Norris mean by 'artificially bored' (l. 31)?
5 Explain the meaning of 'he stood for the ceremonies' (l. 35).
6 Why do you think Donald Davies was sick?
7 Who were Billy Rose's 'executioners' (l. 43)?
8 What does the poet mean by 'the flowers of blood' (l. 47)?
9 What does 'frantic' mean as used in l. 52?
10 Why does the poet speak of 'three treacherous pence', and 'my three sharp coins knocked out his sight'?

Implications

11 What feelings do you think Leslie Norris had about professional boxing by the time he wrote this?
12 Do you think he felt the same way about football? What do you think boxing and football have in common? In what way do the two sports differ?
13 There are dangers in most sports, but which ones depend for their excitement on danger?
14 Should we allow ourselves the pleasure of seeing others injured?
15 How far is boxing 'the noble art of self-defence'?
16 Should boys be taught boxing? Should boys or girls be taught judo?

Exercises

17 Is this subject suitable for a poem? Leslie Norris has himself explained how he might have written this as a short story instead of

a poem. What do you think was gained by his deciding to write it as a ballad?

18 Describe the crowd arriving to see a match. Decide on your viewpoint—either write as if you had been an observer in a particular vantage point, or as if you had been one of the crowd.

19 Suppose you have to speak either in defence of or against one of these subjects:
a Boxing should be illegal.
b It is better to watch good professional sport than to take part in poor amateur sport.
List your points for, or against. Write them into a speech.

20 Write a ballad of your own about one of the following:
a a professional sportsman or woman.
b an accident in sport.
c the flowers of blood.

¶ *What things have you enjoyed doing in your own time that have nevertheless been uncomfortable? Why did you do them?*

¶ *Have your own pursuits ever led you into danger?*

¶ *How would you enjoy a life free from all danger and discomfort?*

Elvin's Rides

Lampang was the end of the road.

From Lampang to Lampoon we had to cycle by the side of the railway. It was eighty kilometres.

We went to Lampang station, hugged a path that ran by it for three hundred yards, mounted a high bridge which ran by the railway, crossed it with meticulous care, it being of open rafters, then sloped down with the lines to the track and set off at the edge for Come What May.

In an instant we were happy. Arterial, modern and cement roads are not for bicycles; it's the little ways where the bike comes into its own: the tracks by canals, jungle or forest ways, country lanes or, as here now, by the side of a railway. This ride was not to prove all as easy as the beginning but it was to be an eighty kilometres run to be cherished in the memory.

Sadly, after six kilometres the track began tricks. From a foot wide it lessened to three inches, with an incline to the left and a raised flint track to the right. Then the three inches began to tilt, even to a dangerous 20 degrees so that a person had to cycle like lightning to remain upright.

Ramesh had many small falls but it was I who had the mighty one. I was well ahead and had my three-inch track, which at that moment was like a three-inch ribbon on a twelve-inch wall, there being a big drop to my left and the high raised track to my right. The three-inch ribbon began to sink as if the earth had given way under a tramway line, so that soon, since the wheels were sinking with the tracks, the pedals would not have height enough to turn. I hoped all would right itself and I worked up a speed, thinking to free-wheel till a better stretch. Then, with me at high speed, the little ribbon sank awfully and I saw that the pedals even half up, which is the extreme free-wheeling height, would be jammed. I could not stop, there was no space on either side on which to dismount. I had to spring either way. I knew if I fell while on Sir Walter, my weight would buckle both wheels, so I would have to throw myself. The hard metal rails and the cruel flints looked the worst of the story, so I chose the sloping bank. I yelled to Ramesh so that he could stop long in advance, then I flung myself in true Rugby football style, slack in all limbs, roly-polying down the long incline. A few cuts, no hurt from the tumble and Sir Walter upright above me wondering why its rider had suddenly become so undignified.

That was the danger of this ride: that, for half of it, dismounting for any reason was impossible; and the reasons for needing to dismount could be: a train, a buffalo across the track, a broken piece of line pitched down, treacherous sand or gravel surface, or even the fading out altogether of that three-inch ribbon so that there was nothing else left to ride on. When no cycling was possible we had to push our cycles over the flint ways between the rails, often pot-holed and at times over small bridges with open rafters. This was the hell of it, this pushing. And with no knowledge of the time-tables it was dangerous too as a train might appear at any moment and run us down like 'a grasshopper on the railroad track'.

Sir Walter and I are great friends. But only when riding. When at-the-push we loathe each other. Often, thrusting it from sleeper to sleeper, pits of sand would bog the wheels down and under the merciless sun the effort became grim.

We had only gone a few kilometres after the fifth station down the line when a khaki figure stopped us in the middle of the track. He had a revolver and a cartridge belt at his waist.

'Where do you think you are going?'

'Do you speak English?'

'I speak a little. Where are you going?'

'From Lampang to Lampoon by the side of the railway.'

'You have come from Lampang through the woods and the hills?'

'Yes, through the woods and the hills.'

'Do you know that they are the fifty kilometres of the most bandit-riddled territory in the whole of Asia?'

'Blimey.'

'Are you a bandit?' asked Ramesh.

'I am a policeman in charge of this area. No one ever did this: no foreigner: no European. You had better come home and I will tell you some things.'

So off we went with the Law.

He had a lovely wife who began making us coffee. She was slight: light in weight as thistledown, light in colour as the kernel of almonds. 'I would be frightened to touch her', said Ramesh. 'She would come to pieces in my fingers.'

The Law would have scared us if we had had to retrace our steps; as it was it mystified us to find that such a peaceful innocent ride had been through bandit-thick area.

'What about from here to Lampoon?' we asked.

'You are out of it now. Those hills a little way back finish the bandits' lines of activity. From now to Chiengmai is completely safe. But I will give you a note to every station-master till Lampoon so that one can ring another up in case you do become overdue.'

Ramesh was longing to be photographed with the policeman's wife and didn't understand how anyone could talk of anything with this new-found female wonder around.

HAROLD ELVIN

Questions

1 What does 'meticulous' mean here (l. 6)? Why did they cross the bridge with 'meticulous care'?

2 Why does the author say 'it's the little ways where the bike comes into its own' (l. 10)?

3 What tricks was the track playing on the two riders even before Elvin's fall?

LEISURE

4 Why did Elvin have to stop pedalling?
5 Who is Sir Walter?
6 What dangers were involved in pushing the bikes?
7 How long was the journey from Lampang to Lampoon? How far had they gone when they met the policeman?
8 Why was the policeman surprised to see them?
9 What steps did the policeman take to protect them on the rest of their way?
10 Why would the rest of the journey be less dangerous for the riders even without the policeman's precautions?

Implications

11 What can you tell about Elvin's companion?
12 What did Elvin gain by making his journey on a bicycle instead of by train? What inconveniences did he suffer?
13 What does a tourist miss when in a party on an organised trip?
14 Why do so many people take their holidays abroad?
15 Do you think people should get well away from home when on holiday, or should they try to enjoy their own home area more?
16 People do not all want to spend their leisure in the same way. What can we tell about a person from the way in which he or she spends leisure time? Does this tell us any more or less than does the way in which they work?

Exercises

17 Write a composition about one of the following:
 a Off the beaten track.
 b My worst journey.
 c Difficult cycling.
 d The time I chose danger.

18 With the help of an atlas, work out the route of the longest overland journey you would like to make. Write down the names of countries you would pass through and then say what would be your main difficulties and what you would most look forward to.

19 List the points you would make in favour of holiday travel (*a*) on foot, (*b*) by bicycle, (*c*) with a coach party, (*d*) by car.

20 Write a letter to a friend to persuade him or her to join you on a holiday. Explain the difficulties, dangers and rewards you might expect while away.

21 Put yourself in the place of the policeman who met Harold Elvin and Ramesh. Write out an official report of what took place and the action you took.

Discussion and Writing

Photograph No. 6 (facing page 67)

Would it be unusual to see this game being played in London? Why do you think these people are playing it? What are the other people there doing? Are they showing any interest?

Imagine you are the woman with the dog: write down, as in a diary, what she has seen and done while out in the park that day.

Write about any unorganised sport you enjoy.

7 Communicating (How can we know?)

¶ Can you remember a headline in a paper you have seen today or in the last few days? Did you read any further? Was the rest of the article as interesting or exciting as the headline?

¶ What paper do you see most often? What interests you most in it? What least?

Scoop

[*Scoop* is a novel about journalists.]

William returned home with a mission; he was going to do down Benito. Love, patriotism, zeal for justice, and personal spite flamed within him as he sat at his typewriter and began his message. One finger was not enough; he used both hands. The keys rose together like bristles on a porcupine, jammed and were extricated; curious anagrams appeared on the paper before him; vulgar fractions and marks of punctuation mingled with the letters. Still he typed.

The wireless station closed at nine; at five minutes to William pushed his sheaf of papers over the counter.

'Two thousand words from Boot,' said Mr Salter.
'Any good?' asked the general editor.
'Look at it.'
The general editor looked. He saw 'Russian plot . . . coup d'état . . . overthrow constitutional government . . . red dictatorship . . . goat butts head of police . . . imprisoned blonde . . . vital British interest jeopardised'. It was enough; it was news. 'It's news,' he said. 'Stop the machines at Manchester and Glasgow. Clear the line to Belfast and Paris. Scrap the whole front page. Kill the Ex-Beauty Queen's pauper funeral. Get in a photograph of Boot.'
'I don't suppose we've got a photograph of Boot in the office.'
'Ring up his relatives. Find his best girl. There must be a photograph of him somewhere in the world.'
'They took one for his passport,' said Mr Salter doubtfully, 'but I remember thinking at the time it was an extremely poor likeness.'
'I don't care if it looks like a baboon——'
'That's just how it does look.'

'Give it two columns' depth. This is the first front page foreign news we've had for a month.'

When the final edition had left the machines, carrying William's sensational message into two million apathetic homes, Mr Salter left the office.

EVELYN WAUGH

Questions

1 What were William Boot's four motives for typing his despatch?
2 How can we tell that Boot is an inexperienced journalist?
3 How carefully does the general editor read Boot's report? What is he looking for?
4 What clear facts, if any, caught the general editor's eye?
5 What would you say was the most serious point noticed by the general editor in Boot's report?
6 What is meant by 'Kill the Ex-Beauty Queen's pauper funeral' (l. 18)?
7 Why was the general editor so anxious to splash Boot's story on the front page?
8 What does 'apathetic' mean here (l. 30)? What does the author imply in saying that the papers carried 'William's sensational message into two million apathetic homes' (l. 29)?
9 Is there anything in the passage to indicate the general editor's concern for publishing the truth?
10 What is the meaning of the book's title?

Implications

11 Judging by the items in William Boot's report that caught the general editor's attention, what sort of thing obviously made news in his paper? Which one word in this extract from *Scoop* sums this up?
12 Why was the general editor anxious to show a photo of Boot? How important is it for readers to know all about the reporters who supply the news for their paper?
13 'It was enough; it was news' (l. 16). What is 'news'? What sorts of news should newspapers supply?
14 As we claim to have a free press, should newspaper editors be free to print whatever they like?

15 Is news broadcast on television and radio in any way different from news as presented in your newspaper?

Exercises

16 *a* List, in order of priority, the subjects that you think a newspaper should cover.
b Take two or more daily papers (preferably for the same day). Write down for each the amount of space, in column inches, given to each subject on your list.

17 Imagine you are a reporter about to interview either the Minister of Education, or of Transport, or of Defence. Draw up a list of questions that you would use as a basis for your interview.

18 Write a letter to your daily or local paper suggesting that certain kinds of news need fuller coverage.

19 Take five headlines from a newspaper and rewrite them at full length so as to bring out their exact meaning.

20 (This could be done in conjunction with Exercise 16, and might require group work.)
In the same evening, make a note of the news items introduced in the news services of B.B.C. Television, I.T.A., and B.B.C. sound. Keep to the order in which the items were presented. Compare results to see which items were given prominence by the different news services.

¶ *Have you ever signed a hire-purchase agreement? If so, did you read it right through?*

¶ *What are the advantages of paying by instalment? What are the snags?*

¶ *How can you check the claims made for a product in an advertisement?*

Death of a Salesman

LINDA: And Willy, don't forget to ask for a little advance, because we've got the insurance premium. It's the grace period now.
WILLY: That's a hundred . . . ?

LINDA: A hundred and eight, sixty-eight. Because we're a little short again.
WILLY: Why are we short?
LINDA: Well, you had the motor job on the car. . . .
WILLY: That goddam Studebaker!
LINDA: And you got one more payment on the refrigerator. . . .
WILLY: But it just broke again!
LINDA: Well, it's old, dear.
WILLY: I told you we should've bought a well-advertised machine. Charley bought a General Electric and it's twenty years old and it's still good, that son-of-a-bitch.
LINDA: But, Willy——
WILLY: Whoever heard of a Hastings refrigerator? Once in my life I would like to own something outright before it's broken! I'm always in a race with the junkyard! I just finished paying for the car and it's on its last legs. The refrigerator consumes belts like a goddam maniac. They time those things. They time them so when you finally paid for them they're used up.
LINDA (*buttoning up his jacket as he unbuttons it*): All told, about two hundred dollars would carry us, dear. But that includes the last payment on the mortgage. After this payment, Willy, the house belongs to us.
WILLY: It's twenty-five years!
LINDA: Biff was nine years old when we bought it.
WILLY: Well, that's a great thing. To weather a twenty-five-year mortgage is——
LINDA: It's an accomplishment.
WILLY: All the cement, the lumber, the reconstruction I put in this house! There ain't a crack to be found in it any more.
LINDA: Well, it served its purpose.
WILLY: What purpose? Some stranger'll come along, move in, and that's that. If only Biff would take this house, and raise a family. . . . (*He starts to go.*) Good-bye, I'm late.

ARTHUR MILLER

Questions

1 What is a Studebaker? Why does Willy curse his?

2 Why does Willy object to paying the final instalment on the refrigerator?

3   What brand of refrigerator do Willy and Linda have? Why does Willy regret having that make?

4   Explain what Willy means by 'I'm always in a race with the junkyard' (l. 18).

5   'They time those things' (l. 20). What does Willy mean by 'they'?

6   How many hire-purchase payments is Willy due to make and what are they on?

7   What is Willy most proud of about his house?

8   Why does he feel this pride and purpose have come to nothing?

9   How long have Willy and Linda been paying for their home?

10   Now that the house is nearly his own, what is Willy's chief complaint?

Implications

11   Willy wishes he had bought 'a well-advertised' refrigerator. Does a well-known manufacturer's name carry reliability?

12   What advantage had hire-purchase been to Willy and Linda?

13   Would you rather rent a house or buy your own by paying off a mortgage in instalments?

14   Should manufactured goods have a guaranteed length of life?

Exercises

15   *a*   List the questions you would like to have answered before buying (i) a car, or (ii) a refrigerator, or (iii) a television set.
b   Collect advertisements for different makes of each and say how many of your questions find their answers in each advertisement.
c   Say what was most striking about each advertisement and whether this had anything to do with any of your questions.

16   Write a letter to a manufacturer or dealer complaining that an article you have bought under guarantee is faulty.

17   Rewrite the second half of this scene, from LINDA (*buttoning up his jacket* . . .), as if it were in a novel; OR in pairs, try improvising a further conversation between Willy and Linda—for example, over supper at the end of the day.

¶ Has a book, play, or film ever stirred you into forgetting that it was 'unreal'?

¶ Can there be any truth in a play or story that is based on true events but alters facts for dramatic reasons?

¶ What film or play has aroused your strongest feelings?

Except the Lord

I don't suppose anyone nowadays knows the story of Maria Marten or The Murder in the Red Barn, or has seen any of the scores of plays founded upon it. An actual murder, I believe, did take place about 1830. It arose, I am told, from the sordid enough liaison of a dissolute farmer's son with a village girl who was already the mother of several illegitimate children. This unsavoury Lothario killed his paramour when she attempted to blackmail him into marriage, ran away to London, was quickly traced, arrested and duly hanged. The case owed its celebrity, apparently, to one sole circumstance; the girl's mother, Mrs Marten, testified at the trial that she had seen in a dream both the murderer and the burial place of the body in one of Corder's barns called the Red Barn.

In fact, Maria's body was found buried in the barn, and this discovery led to Corder's arrest.

I say that the story was sordid enough. Corder was a common type of village blackguard, and Maria Marten a girl of loose character. But the play of the evening, like, I believe, all the popular versions then in circulation, was very different. Maria on the stage became the virtuous child of poor cottagers, and Corder a rich gentleman, son of the squire who was the Martens' landlord; his liaison with Maria was no longer a common intrigue with the village Jezebel, but a deliberate seduction by a villain. One might say, indeed, that it was rape; for Corder, as we saw him that evening, forced Maria to surrender by threatening to raise her father's rent by an impossible amount, and to evict him if he did not pay.

That is to say, the drama we saw, and that millions had seen, was a story of the cruellest kind of wrong inflicted by the rich upon the poor. Throughout the play everything possible was done to show the virtue, innocence and helplessness of the poor, and the abandoned cruelty, the heartless self-indulgence of the rich.

And this was one among hundreds of such plays. I have wondered often how such propaganda failed to bring to England also, as to

France, Italy, Germany, almost every other nation, a bloody revolution. For its power was incredible. As I say, it was decisive in my own life.

With what heart-moving sympathy I watched the poor village girl as the brute Corder marked her down for ruin. I knew also the power of the landlord to oppress, and the weakness of poverty in self-defence. I wanted to cry out a warning, and when Corder himself appeared, the very picture of arrogant wealth, how I hated him. Hatred is far too mild a term for a feeling which would not have been satisfied merely to kill. I longed to see him torn to pieces, to be tortured to death.

I was trembling all over. My face was wet with tears and sweat. I heard myself utter groans and smothered cries. It was all I could do not to shout out my sympathy and my rage. In fact, cries of anger and exclamations of horror did continually break out from the audience throughout the whole performance. The women, especially, gave vent to their feelings. The old wife who had admitted me to the ropes never stopped muttering to herself, 'Ah, poor thing—poor old man—listen to the brute, and he a gentleman born.' One girl, also near the ropes, broke into loud hysterical sobs.

I suppose no one in that tent, however inexperienced and ignorant, failed to realise that the play was a made-up thing, an artful construction whose whole object was to work upon our feelings. Yet our feelings were stirred more violently than by any truth, by any tragedy of our own lives.

But how is it possible for me to convey the effect of dramatic art upon one who had never seen such a thing before, who had never, for instance, seen even amateur theatricals, or a school performance? I have heard it said that a man's first experience in the theatre opens a new world to him—it would be better to say that it destroys the old one. That half-hour in the booth at Lilmouth, crowded among farm labourers at the rope which alone divided us from the strange beings of the stage with their flaring paint and loud voices, their bold gestures, was a decisive event in my life and, I believe, in Georgina's.

And why in retrospect should I be astonished at such events? Is there not an element of drama still not only in our churches, but in the ritual of government? You may be sure that what has survived for centuries in spite of criticism has powerful motives for existence. Believe me, art, and especially the drama, above all the popular drama, has a fearful power and responsibility in the world—it acts directly upon the very centres of feeling and passion.

For me Maria was an epitome of helpless innocence and simplicity; and when her murderer stood before me, actually in that small space, within a few feet of me, my heart seemed to falter at the terror of such guilt. How, I felt, could any human being commit such villainies and stand there before a crowd of his fellows and own it—act it?

80 And I felt these overwhelming emotions although I was perfectly aware that Maria was an actress performing a part, and that Corder was merely a poor player whose livelihood it was to give any representation required of him.

Still stranger and more terrible truth, even in the midst of my horror at this monster in his blood guilt, I was aware of a fascinated admiration. When in his soliloquies at the front of the stage, his eyes, roving over the audience, seemed to meet mine, they sent forth an indescribable thrill—it seemed that something flashed from the very centre of evil into my deepest soul.

JOYCE CARY

Questions

1 What made the true story of Maria Marten seem sordid to the writer?

2 The main facts of this crime were not unusual. What made the case of Maria Marten seem out of the ordinary?

3 How did the play differ from the true case?

4 What political or class bias did the play give to the story?

5 Whom did the audience sympathise with during the performance?

6 How did the audience show its response to the actors?

7 Which words show that watching this performance altered the course of the writer's life?

8 Where else in daily life does drama work upon people's strong feelings, according to the writer?

9 What did Maria seem to the writer to represent or symbolise?

10 What contradictory feelings did the writer feel on the one hand for Corder as a character, and on the other hand for the actor playing him?

Implications

11 From this piece of writing can we tell anything about the writer's social position?

7

8

12 The author was describing country people who could not have known film or television and who seldom, if ever, saw live actors. Their reactions, as a result, were strong and demonstrative. Can you remember seeing a play or a film that aroused strong reactions from those watching? Were these reactions visible, audible, or merely felt privately?

13 The writer of this account embarked on a career as a political orator. What do you think he owed to the experience of seeing *Maria Marten*?

14 Do you think politicians appearing on television have to be able to act to some extent? Is it fair to judge a party political speaker by his performance on television?

Exercises

15 Write an account of the most impressive performance you have seen by an actor or speaker.

16 Write a scene for a play (to be staged or televised) which introduces a tenant family and a landlord or his agent.

17 Divide a page down the centre. On one side make a list of the facts known about the real story of Maria Marten, and opposite to them note the changes, if any, that these facts underwent in the play.

18 Write on the subject of The Spellbinders.

Discussion and Writing

Photograph No. 7 (facing page 82)

Is this old lady the paper-seller? What is she herself reading about? What is attracting the attention of the three children?

Write down for the old woman and the boy in turn, what has caught their attention in the paper, and what their reactions are.

Write a poem called 'Read All About It'.

8 Education

¶ Who needs education?

¶ Now that you are at or near the end of your school life, do you feel that you have had the sort of schooling you would have liked? How would you want the schooling of any children you may have to differ from that you received?

¶ When do you reckon you will have learnt all you need to know? Is this the same as asking 'When will your education finish?'

The History of Mr Polly

I remember seeing a picture of Education—in some place. I think it was Education, but quite conceivably it represented the Empire teaching her Sons, and I have a strong impression that it was a wallpainting upon some public building in Manchester or Birmingham or Glasgow, but very possibly I am mistaken about that. It represented a glorious woman, with a wise and fearless face, stooping over her children, and pointing them to far horizons. The sky displayed the pearly warmth of a summer dawn, and all the painting was marvellously bright, as if with the youth and hope of the delicately beautiful children in the foreground. She was telling them, one felt, of the great prospect of life that opened before them, of the splendours of sea and mountain they might travel and see, the joys of skill they might acquire, of effort and the pride of effort, and the devotions and nobilities it was theirs to achieve. Perhaps even she whispered of the warm triumphant mystery of love that comes at last to those who have patience and unblemished hearts....

The education of Mr Polly did not follow this picture very closely. He went for some time to a National School, which was run on severely economical lines to keep down the rates, by a largely untrained staff; he was set sums to do that he did not understand, and that no one made him understand; he was made to read the Catechism and Bible with the utmost industry and an entire disregard of punctuation or significance; caused to imitate writing copies and drawing copies; given object lessons upon sealing-wax and silkworms and potato bugs and ginger, and iron and such-like things; taught various other subjects his mind refused to entertain; and afterwards, when he was about twelve, he was jerked by his parents to 'finish off' in a private school of dingy aspect and still dingier pretensions, where there were no object lessons, and the studies of book-keeping and French were pursued (but never effectually overtaken) under the guidance of an elderly gentleman, who wore a nondescript gown and took snuff, wrote copperplate, explained nothing, and used a cane with remarkable dexterity and gusto.

Mr Polly went into the National School at six, and he left the private school at fourteen, and by that time his mind was in much the same state that you would be in, dear reader, if you were operated upon for appendicitis by a well-meaning, boldly enterprising, but rather overworked and underpaid butcher boy, who was superseded towards the climax of the operation by a left-handed clerk of high principles but intemperate habits—that is to say, it was in a thorough mess. The nice little curiosities and willingness of a child were in a jumbled and thwarted condition, hacked and cut about—the operators had left, so to speak, all their sponges and ligatures in the mangled confusion—and Mr Polly had lost much of his natural confidence, so far as figures and sciences and languages and the possibilities of learning things were concerned. He thought of the present world no longer as a wonderland of experiences, but as geography and history, as the repeating of names that were hard to pronounce, and lists of products and populations and heights and lengths, and as lists and dates—oh! and Boredom indescribable.

But the indigestions of mind and body that were to play so large a part in his subsequent career were still only beginning. His liver and his gastric juice, his wonder and imagination kept up a fight against the things that threatened to overwhelm soul and body together. Outside the regions devastated by the school curriculum he was intensely curious. He had cheerful phases of enterprise, and about thirteen he suddenly discovered reading and its joys. He began to read stories voraciously, and books of travel, provided they were also adventurous. He got these chiefly from the local institute, and he also 'took in' irregularly, but thoroughly, one of those inspiring weeklies that dull people used to call 'penny dreadfuls', admirable weeklies crammed with imagination that the cheap boys' 'comics' of today have replaced. At fourteen, when he emerged from the valley of the shadow of education, there survived something, indeed it survived still, obscured and thwarted, at five-and-thirty, that pointed—not with a visible and prevailing finger like the finger of that beautiful woman in the picture, but pointed nevertheless—to the idea that there was interest and happiness in the world. Deep in the being of Mr Polly, deep in that darkness, like a creature which has been beaten about the head and left for dead but still lives, crawled a persuasion that over and above the things that are jolly and 'bits of all right' there was beauty, there was delight; that somewhere—magically inaccessible perhaps, but still somewhere—were pure and easy and joyous states of body and mind.

He would read tales about hunters and explorers, and imagine himself riding mustangs as fleet as the wind across the prairies of Western America, or coming as a conquering and adored white man into the swarming villages of Central Africa. He shot bears with a revolver—a cigarette in the other hand—and made a necklace of their teeth and claws for the chief's beautiful daughter. Also, he killed a lion with a pointed stake, stabbing through the beast's heart as it stood over him.

Engaged in these pursuits he would neglect the work immediately in hand, sitting somewhere slackly on the form and projecting himself in a manner tempting to a schoolmaster with a cane. . . . And twice he had books confiscated.

Recalled to the realities of life, he would rub himself or sigh as the occasion required, and resume his attempts to write as good as copperplate. He hated writing; the ink always crept up his fingers, and the smell of ink offended him. And he was filled with unexpressed doubts. Why should writing slope down from right to left? Why should downstrokes be thick and upstrokes thin? Why should the handle of one's pen point over one's right shoulder?

His copy books towards the end foreshadowed his destiny and took the form of commercial documents. 'Dear Sir,' they ran, 'Referring to your esteemed order of the 26th ult., we beg to inform you,' and so on.

The compression of Mr Polly's mind and soul in the educational institutions of his time was terminated abruptly by his father, between his fourteenth and fifteenth birthday. His father—who had long since forgotten the time when his little son's limbs seemed to have come straight from God's hand, and when he had kissed five minute toe-nails in a rapture of loving tenderness—remarked—

'It's time that dratted boy did something for a living.'

And a month or so later Mr Polly began that career in business that led him at last to the sole proprietorship of a bankrupt outfitter's shop.

H. G. WELLS

Questions

1 What is Wells's main criticism of Mr Polly's schooling?

2 Polly was 'taught various other subjects his mind refused to entertain' (l. 26). How would you say this in your own words?

3 'The nice little curiosities and willingness of a child' (l. 41). Has a child of about six, or just over, got curiosity and willingness? Think of children you know.

4 Why did 'books of travel' (l. 58) in particular appeal to Polly?

5 What was a 'penny dreadful' (l. 61)?

6 In spite of his education 'there survived . . . something that pointed' (l. 64) for Polly. Can you say what this something pointed to for him?

7 Mr Polly was recalled from day dreams 'to the realities of life' (l. 88). What were these 'realities'? Were they, or are they, really the realities of life?

8 'His copy books towards the end foreshadowed his destiny' (l. 95). What destiny was this sort of education preparing him for?

9 'He was filled with unexpressed doubts' (l. 91). What sort of doubts were these, and why did they remain unexpressed?

10 Was Mr Polly's father being heartless or practical when he remarked, 'It's time that dratted boy did something for a living' (l. 105)?

Implications

11 Which parts of the picture of education have little or nothing to do with education as you know it today?

12 What is the meaning of 'Referring to your esteemed order of the 26th ult., we beg to inform you . . .'? Why was a business letter worded in that way?

13 In your own experience of school, what has been most likely to bore you?

14 Can you say why you were bored? Can you suggest ways in which this boredom might have been avoided or reduced? How much of the boredom was a necessary evil?

15 Do you think education should do any more than prepare you for a career or job?

Exercises

16 If you had to design a mural representing 'Education for the Future', what would your picture show?

17 Write a letter opening with your translation of Polly's exercise. It should be from you as secretary of a firm in answer to a client who has ordered an article that you manufacture, e.g. a typewriter, or a washing machine, or an electric drill, or a record player.

18 List five books, giving title and author, that you have read and could recommend to anyone in a similar state of boredom to that of Alfred Polly.

¶ *Should your schooling help you to find a job that suits you?*

¶ *After you have left school, is there any point in keeping contact with it? If so, why? And what sort of contact would it be?*

Hurry on Down

[Charles Lumley, who recently left university, decides to take up window-cleaning and calls on the Headmaster of his old grammar school for help.]

A contract! The holy word echoed through his mind as he clambered out of the bus in the market square and walked up the hill to the school.

Complete and joyous as his rejection of the past had been, he still could not walk into the ivy-clad red building—a fake Rugby like so many minor schools of its period—with the sang-froid of one who had never been there before. Although the eight years he had spent here were part of a former life, that former life had the power, at least, to cause him discomfort enough to pierce his new-found calm. To be recognised by the janitor; to be conducted, in the afternoon drowsiness, down the corridor past that row of dingy form rooms where the pitiful farce of his childhood had been played out act after endless act, and where the dragons, gods, and wizards who had peopled that fantastic region sat now, even this minute, building their endless crumbling structure in the minds of a fresh generation. It was uncomfortable; but the discomfort dropped away when he was left alone in the headmaster's waiting-room, for with solitude returned the consciousness that he had cut away the tentacles that bound him to the kind of life that this place represented. So soon after his seed-time, he was here to ask for a limited and definite harvest. A contract!

At last he was ushered into the headmaster's study: that room which, with its careful arrangement of the 'traditional' props of leather armchairs, classical busts, glass-fronted bookcases, had been the scene of the utmost disasters and triumphs of his boyhood, though he had been too average a boy to enter it more than four or five times during his eight years. And there was the familiar sardonic face wryly hovering behind its thick lenses.

'Well now, Lumley; and what can I,' here he paused for an instant, and spoke the next three words with unnecessary distinctness, as if to parody them, 'do for you?'

'You could look straight at me, to start with,' Charles almost replied, for Scrodd was up to his usual game of peering ironically in his direction, vaguely taking in with his short-sighted glance the general area within which his interlocutor might be found, like one who has seen a tiny insect on the wallpaper, lost it again, and is half-interestedly looking for it. But annoyed as he felt at this habitual, perfunctory insolence, he refrained from any sign of impatience, for, in the three years during which he and Scrodd had not met, he had become familiar with the peculiar psychological burden under which the schoolmaster was sinking. He could read the bland imbecile like a newspaper: the early ambitions, the resolve to apply half his energies to his ordinary duties and half to the studies that were to lead him to the limelight, and finally the fading of his dreams, leaving him rigidly set in a travesty of his original position, with half his attention focused on whatever he was doing or whomever he was talking to, and the other half feebly glinting out from the paralysed area of his mind, focused, with terrible obstinacy, on nothing.

'I thought you might be so kind as to help me professionally, sir,' Charles said briskly.

Scrodd gave a slight twitch that brought his wandering gaze to within three inches of Charles's shoulder. A sneer appeared on his face.

'I could have saved you trouble, Lumley, if you had mentioned in your letter what it was you wanted to see me about: I could have told you that this school is fully staffed, and that I have no influence elsewhere.'

Charles leaned forward in incredulous pity. The scarecrow actually thought that he, a free human being, wished to enrol in his shambling regiment of pedagogues.

'My intention is not to enter the teaching profession, Mr Scrodd. My vocational requirements are,' he hesitated, 'simpler and easier to fulfil.'

For a moment, as he faced the enormity of the task in hand, Charles felt a renewal of his old confusion, guilt, and blankness. His tongue stiffened so as to choke all utterance, and he became the same ludicrously insecure figure he had been during all his previous visits to that study. Then, immediately, the mists cleared, and the sanity he had so dearly bought swept him forward on its powerful current until his feet were once more on solid ground.

'And in what way,' demanded Scrodd insolently, looking ironically past him, 'are they easy for me to fulfil?'

Charles leaned back in his chair, and fixed his eyes on the thick lenses opposite.

'This school has windows. Someone must have to clean them from time to time; either someone from outside, or one of the school servants who could be better employed about his ordinary duties. Now this, as you yourself once remarked to me, is the age of the specialist.'

Scrodd seemed to have fallen into a trance: his eyes were groping in Charles's direction as if searching for an invisible opponent.

'So why not give the job regularly to one of your old boys? I could make a journey over here, without any reminding, say at the beginning or end of each term, and make a couple of days' job of it, and of course my charges would——'

Scrodd was on his feet, and the miracle had happened. He was looking directly at Charles.

'I am still hoping,' he articulated distinctly, 'that this will turn out to be some foolish joke on your part.'

'——be less than whatever it is you're having to pay now.'

'Perhaps a touch of the sun. It has been hot lately.'

'Look at it this way. Suppose you don't get anyone in from outside, who is there who can do it decently? No one. Smith's too fat and rheumatic to get to the top of a ladder, and as for Bert, you must know that he can't be spared from the coke-shovelling——'

'Lumley! Spare me the trouble of ringing for the janitor and having you taken out of here by force!'

'——except during the summer, and then he has to act as groundsman. I could take the whole thing off their hands, and make the windows a credit to the school.'

Scrodd's hand jerked to the bell, and pressed the button, holding it feverishly down. Charles stood up. He had about one minute, the time it would take Smith to plod back down the corridor, in which to say his last words to Scrodd. It was inconceivable that they should ever meet again. And yet he had not the slightest urge to say anything, either cutting, furious, or conciliatory. The time for summaries was over. He had no breath to spare for his past life and its debris.

Oddly, it was Scrodd who felt the need to elaborate.

'I can only conclude, Lumley, that you felt some kind of grudge against me that impelled you to come back and waste my time with this foolish joke. Window cleaning! I suppose the implication is that your education had unfitted you for anything worth doing, and you seek to drive the point home by coming here with this foolish talk about having turned artisan. You need not have spoken in parable.'

Charles turned away as Smith opened the door. He felt no wish to comment on Scrodd's reading of the case. He merely said, over his shoulder, 'Why not in parable? I spent eight years here being taught to think metaphorically.'

And as Smith held the door for him to go out, he broke suddenly into the drowsy quiet of the corridor with a rendering, as musical as he could make it, of his obsessive fragment:

> 'May their seed-time past be yielding
> Year by year a richer store!'

Smith, scandalised, hustled him down the service stairs and out into the sunshine.

JOHN WAIN

Questions

1 Who are the 'dragons, gods, and wizards' (l. 13)? Why does Charles refer to them in this way?

2 What does Charles Lumley feel about the eight years spent at his school? How is this made clear before he ever reaches the headmaster's room?

3 How also can we tell that Charles is not entirely at ease on re-entering his old school?

4 What do the words 'its careful arrangement of the "traditional" props' (l. 23) tell us about the headmaster?

5 Charles first asks the headmaster to help him professionally. From Scrodd's reply, what do you think he took this to mean?

6 How is it clear that after his first confidence, Charles is afraid of coming to the point of his request to Scrodd?

7 Charles's offer was a serious one; was it a reasonable one?

8 Why is Scrodd so outraged?

9 Why does Charles break into song as he goes?

10 Why does Charles think Scrodd a failure as a schoolmaster?

Implications

11 In what ways does John Wain make Scrodd seem absurd?

12 In what other ways does the author make this whole episode comic? If it is meant to be comic can it also be serious?

13 Does the episode correspond in any way with what might happen in real life?

14 From Scrodd's indignation that an old pupil should be satisfied with being a window-cleaner what do we learn about (*a*) Scrodd himself, and (*b*) his aims as a teacher?

15 If you can see why Charles thinks Scrodd a failure, say what sort of teacher he might think of as a success.

Exercises

16 Imagine you are a schoolteacher and write the diary of one day in your term-time life.

17 Imagine you have left school and wish to see your old headmaster to ask for help in your work. Write a letter to him asking for an appointment and stating your reasons.

18 Write a short description of the sort of school Charles Lumley went to, as if you were Scrodd, its headmaster.

19 In a paragraph describe one of the following:
  a your headmaster's study,
  b the school office,
  c your doctor's waiting-room,
  d the foyer of a cinema or theatre that you know.

¶ *Should pupils have a say in the way their school is run? Is there any way in which this could be done regularly and constructively?*

¶ *Have you ever spoken to a whole hall full of people? Or even to more than ten people together? How might it help you after leaving school, to have spoken to an audience as part of school training?*

To Sir, With Love

[A teacher describes an event in the life of his school in East London.]

The half-yearly report of the Students' Council was on November 15th, and was one of the important days in the calendar of Greenslade School. I had heard quite a deal about these occasions and became as excited as the children as the day approached. It was entirely their day, arranged, presented and controlled by them. I observed the activities of my class as they prepared for it, noting with pride the business-like way in which tasks were allocated and fitted into a neat programme. There were whispered conferences with members of other classes in the arrangement of it.

On that day there was no assembly. The children arrived smartly dressed and polished, and Miss Joseph and Denham, who seemed to be the important officials for the occasion, moved about among their colleagues ensuring that each one was ready to play his (or her) part.

A bell was rung at 10 a.m. and everyone trooped into the auditorium to sit together in classes. Miss Joseph and Denham, the two most senior students, sat on the stage, one on each side of Mr Florian, the Headmaster who, as soon as everyone was seated and silent, stood and addressed the school.

As I listened I realised that this man was in no way remote from his school; his remarks all showed that he identified himself with it and everyone in it. He then wished them success with the Council Meeting and left the stage to tremendous applause.

Things now moved quickly into gear. First, Miss Joseph stood up, and gave a short explanation of the Council's purpose and its activities. Each class would report, through its representatives, on the studies pursued during the half year which began after Easter, a representative having been chosen for each subject. When all the classes had completed their reports a panel of teachers would be invited to occupy the stage and answer questions from the body of the hall on matters arising out of the various reports. The selection of the panel, as with everything else, was entirely at the discretion of the children and no members of the staff knew either how many or which teachers would be invited to sit.

When the turn of my class came I sat up anxiously. From the list he held in his hand, Denham called out the names of the representatives, together with the subjects on which they would report.

I felt terribly pleased and proud to see the confident courtesy with which Denham used the term 'Miss' in addressing each of the senior girls; I felt sure that this would in itself be something for the younger ones to aim at, a sort of badge of young adulthood. As their names were called they walked up to the stage and took their seats with commendable gravity.

Miss Joseph then gave a short address. She said that their lessons had all had a particular bias towards the brotherhood of Mankind, and that they had been learning through each subject how all mankind was interdependent in spite of geographical location and differences in colour, races and creeds. Then she called on Potter.

Potter went on to speak of the work they had done on weights and measures, of the relationship between the kilogramme and the pound, the metre and the foot. He said that throughout the world one or other of those two methods was either in use or understood, and that it was a symbol of the greater understanding which was being accomplished between peoples.

Sapiano spoke of the study the class had made of pests, especially black rot on wheat, boll weevil on cotton, and the Colorado beetle on potatoes. He showed how many countries had pooled their knowledge and results of research on the behaviour, breeding habits and migration of these pests, and were gradually reducing the threat they represented to these important products.

Miss Pegg and Jackson divided the report on Geography between them. Jackson spoke first on the distribution of mineral deposits and vegetable produce over the earth's surface, how a country rich in one was often deficient in the other; and of the interchange and interdependence which inevitably followed. Miss Pegg dealt with human relationships, stressing the problems facing the post-war world for feeding, clothing and housing its populations. She also made a reference to the thousands of refugees, stateless and unwanted; and to the efforts and programmes of UNICEF.

Fernman as usual had a trump card up his sleeve. When called he made a signal to someone off-stage, and Welsh and Alison appeared bearing a skeleton between them, together with a sort of gallows.

When this arrangement had been set up there was the skeleton hanging from a hook screwed into the top of its skull, gently revolving at the end of a cord. This was somewhat in the nature of comic relief, and the school showed its approval by laughing uproariously. But levity soon evaporated when Fernman began to speak: his voice was clear and precise and he had a strong sense of the dramatic. Calmly he told them that it was a female skeleton; that was a fact and could easily be proved. But he could not say with any assurance whether she had been Chinese or French or German or Greek; nor could he say if she had been brown or white or a mixture of both. And from that, he said, the class had concluded that basically all people were the same; the trimmings might be different but the foundations were all laid out according to the same blueprint. Fernman was wonderful; he had them eating out of his hand.

Miss Dodd reported on the period of History the class had studied—the Reformation in England. She told of the struggles of men of independent spirit against clerical domination and of their efforts to break from established religious traditions. From those early beginnings gradually grew the idea of tolerance for the beliefs and cultures of others, and the now common interest in trying to study and understand those cultures.

Denham's report was a bit of a shock. He severely criticised the general pattern of P.T. and games, emphasising the serious limitations of space obtaining and the effect of that limitation on their games activities. He complained that the P.T. was ill-conceived and pointless, and the routine monotonous; he could see no advantage in doing it; a jolly good game was far better. Apparently he was voicing the opinions of all the boys, for they cheered him loudly.

When the reports were over, Denham called two children at random from the audience and asked them to write the name of each teacher, including the Head, on a slip of paper. These slips were folded and placed in a hat, juggled vigorously, and then withdrawn one by one. The names were called: Mr Weston, Mrs Dale-Evans, Miss Phillips.

Denham and Miss Joseph led the others off the stage and the teachers took their seats, Weston big and bushily untidy between the two women. Then the questioning began.

I believe I would have gone a long way to see what followed; it was an experience which I shall not easily forget.

E. R. BRAITHWAITE

Questions

1 What reasons might Mr Braithwaite have had for feeling 'as excited as the children' (l. 4), or for noting them 'with pride' (l. 7) as they prepared for the Council?

2 '... arranged, presented and controlled by them' (l. 5). What evidence is there of each of these three parts of the pupils' task in holding the Council?

3 How does Mr Braithwaite justify the use of the term 'Miss' for senior girls?

4 What does the author mean by 'took their seats with commendable gravity' (l. 41)?

5 Do you know what UNICEF is? Even if you do not, can you tell from Miss Pegg's report what work UNICEF does?

6 What two good effects did the arrival of Fernman's gallows have, even before he spoke?

7 What reasons did Fernman have for concluding 'that basically all people were the same' (l. 82)?

8 What is meant by 'he had them eating out of his hand' (l. 85)?

9 What is meant by 'tolerance for the beliefs and cultures of others' (l. 90)?

10 In Denham's report, how much is he criticising the school as a building, and how much as an organisation? Has he anything constructive to say?

Implications

11 Why did the Headmaster leave the stage? Was he wise to do so?

12 What, if anything, were the pupils of Greenslade School learning that day?

13 Should pupils be permitted to question their teachers' methods and organisation?

14 Miss Joseph said 'that their lessons had all had a particular bias'. Should a teacher give biased lessons? Is it possible to be totally unbiased? Are certain kinds of bias more acceptable than others?

15 What was Mr Braithwaite's particular bias? How does it appear in the different subject reports?

16 What more is there to teaching than passing over knowledge from teacher to pupil?

17 It has been said that a school should prepare its pupils for life. What does this mean?

In what sense was Greenslade School preparing its pupils 'for life'?

18 As far as you can tell, do you think Mr Braithwaite would have succeeded as a teacher in any other kind of school, say a grammar or a comprehensive school?

19 Do you think it is a good idea that senior girls should be called 'Miss' at school? How do you think senior boys should be addressed?

20 Is there anything in this extract to indicate to you that Mr Braithwaite is, in fact, a Negro?

Exercises

21 Draw up a programme or agenda for this Council Meeting.

22 This whole extract is a report made by the author. Suppose you were reporting for a school newspaper; how would you cover the main facts of what Mr Braithwaite's class contributed to the Council, in no more than 200 words?

23 Take the reported words of any one speaker and then write down what might have been his or her actual words.

24 Write out the report that you might give at such a Council Meeting of your work in any subject, so as to show the value of what you are learning.

25 List five questions that you would like to put to staff representatives at such a meeting if your school were to hold one.

Discussion and Writing

Photograph No. 8 (facing page 83)

There are only fifty years between these two photographs.

What is the most striking difference between them?

What differences can you detect between the two school buildings?

WORK AND LEISURE

What other differences are there between the pictures?

How old would one of the boys from the first group be today? What might his comments be on the two pictures?

Write the old man's comments on looking at the school group that he was in.

Three: The World Community

9 The Citizen

¶ *What is the most important thing a citizen wants to know before voting for a candidate at a local election?*

¶ *What sort of matters does a citizen expect his local council to think about for him? What can he do if he strongly disapproves of their decisions?*

The Moon is Down

[In 1940 the Germans invaded Norway. They were swift and thorough. In one town, seized on the first day, the German commander, Colonel Lanser, meets the town's leader, Mayor Orden, to make his demands.]

The colonel began, 'We want to get along as well as we can. You see, sir, this is more like a business venture than anything else. We need the coal-mine here and the fishing. We will try to get along with just as little friction as possible.'

The Mayor said, 'I have had no news. What about the rest of the country?'

'All taken,' said the colonel. 'It was well planned.'

'Was there no resistance anywhere?'

The colonel looked at him compassionately. 'I wish there had not been. Yes, there was some resistance, but it only caused bloodshed. We had planned very carefully.'

Orden stuck to his point. 'But there was resistance?'

'Yes, but it was foolish to resist. Just as here, it was destroyed instantly. It was sad and foolish to resist.'

Doctor Winter caught some of the Mayor's anxiousness about the point. 'Yes,' he said, 'foolish, but they resisted.'

And Colonel Lanser replied, 'Only a few and they are gone. The people as a whole are quiet.'

Doctor Winter said, 'The people don't know yet what has happened.'

'They are discovering,' said Lanser. 'They won't be foolish again.' He cleared his throat and his voice became brisk. 'Now, sir, I must get to business. I'm really very tired, but before I can sleep I must make my arrangements.' He sat forward in his chair. 'I am more engineer than soldier. This whole thing is more an engineering job than conquest. The coal must come out of the ground and be shipped. We have technicians, but the local people will continue to work the mine. Is that clear? We do not wish to be harsh.'

And Orden said, 'Yes, that's clear enough. But suppose the people do not want to work the mine?'

The colonel said, 'I hope they will want to, because they must. We must have the coal.'

'But if they don't?'

'They must. They are an orderly people. They don't want trouble.' He waited for the Mayor's reply and none came. 'Is that not so, sir?' the colonel asked.

Mayor Orden twisted his chain. 'I don't know, sir. They are orderly under their own government. I don't know how they would be under yours. It is untouched ground, you see. We have built our government over four hundred years.'

The colonel said quickly, 'We know that, and so we are going to keep your government. You will still be the Mayor, you will give the orders, you will penalise and reward. In that way, they will not give trouble.'

Mayor Orden looked at Doctor Winter. 'What are you thinking about?'

'I don't know,' said Doctor Winter. 'It would be interesting to see. I'd expect trouble. This might be a bitter people.'

Mayor Orden said, 'I don't know, either.' He turned to the colonel. 'Sir, I am of this people, and yet I don't know what they will do. Perhaps you know. Or maybe it would be different from anything you know or we know. Some people accept appointed leaders and obey them. But my people have elected me. They made me and they can unmake me. Perhaps they will if they think I have gone over to you. I just don't know.'

The colonel said, 'You will be doing them a service if you keep them in order.'

'A service?'

'Yes, a service. It is your duty to protect them from harm. They will be in danger if they are rebellious. We must get the coal, you see. Our leaders do not tell us how; they order us to get it. But you have your people to protect. You must make them do the work and thus keep them safe.'

Mayor Orden asked, 'But suppose they don't want to be safe?'

'Then you must think for them.'

Orden said, a little proudly, 'My people don't like to have others think for them. Maybe they are different from your people. I am confused, but that I am sure of.'

JOHN STEINBECK

Questions

1 For what reasons, according to Lanser, had the Germans occupied the town?

2 What indications are there of the Mayor's complete surprise at the invasion?

3 Why does Lanser say that resistance was foolish?

4 What co-operation does Lanser want of the local people? Why does he expect them to co-operate?

5 Why does the Mayor have doubts about his people's orderliness?

6 Why does Lanser expect the Mayor to give orders and the people to obey them?

7 How does the Mayor explain his position and authority with his people? How does this differ from Lanser's idea?

8 Why does Lanser think that the Mayor's ordering his people to work will be doing them a service?

9 Why does Mayor Orden object to the suggestion that he should think for his people?

10 What, by contrast, does Mayor Orden think the German people expect of their leaders?

Implications

11 Why did Mayor Orden ask so insistently whether any Norwegians had resisted the German invasion?

12 What did these Norwegians value more highly than their safety?

13   What objection might a Norwegian citizen have made to Lanser's comment that he was engaged more on an engineering job than on conquest?

14   Both Colonel Lanser and Mayor Orden were in positions of authority. How did their authority contrast?

15   Why was Mayor Orden proud to say that his people did not like others to think for them?

Exercises

16   Write down the orders that Colonel Lanser might have received from German High Command before he occupied the town.

17   Colonel Lanser wanted Mayor Orden to tell his people what to do. Write out the proclamation that he expected the Mayor to issue.

18   Imagine that before a local election one party promised to speed up rehousing in your district. This party gains control of the council and then restricts the rehousing scheme. Write to your local paper protesting, and suggesting what action should be taken.

¶ *If you found a friend who had been beaten up by a gang, what would be your feeling towards that gang?*

¶ *If a friend, brother, or father is killed in action, whom do you feel is to blame?*

¶ *What is 'patriotism'?*

Serjeant Musgrave's Dance

[Serjeant Musgrave heads a recruiting party in an English town. Wishing to show them the realities of war, he collects a crowd of townspeople, holds them by training a Gatling gun on them and then shows them a soldier's skeleton.]

(*This scene will gain a great deal from being read aloud.*)

MUSGRAVE: Now I said I'll explain. So listen. (*He points to the skeleton.*) This, up here, was a comrade of mine—of ours. At least, he was till a few months since. He was killed, being there for his duty, in the country I was telling you about, where the regiment is

THE CITIZEN

stationed. It's not right a colony, you know, it's a sort of Protectorate, but British, y'know, British. This, up here, he was walking down a street lateish at night, he'd been to the opera—you've got a choral society in this town, I daresay—well, he was only a soldier, but North Country, he was full of music, so he goes to the opera. And on his way again to camp he was shot in the back. And it's not surprising, neither: there was patriots abroad, anti-British, subversive; like they didn't dare to shoot him to his face. He was daft to be out alone, wasn't he? Out of bounds, after curfew.

ATTERCLIFFE (*with suppressed frenzy*): Get on to the words as matter, serjeant!

MUSGRAVE (*turning on him fiercely*): I'm talking now; you wait your turn! ... So we come to the words as matter. He was the third to be shot that week. He was the fifteenth that month. In the back and all. Add to which he was young, he was liked, he sang songs, they say, and he joked and he laughed—he was a good soldier, too, else I'd not have bothered (we'll leave out his sliding off to the opera WOL, but by and large good, and I've got standards). So at twelve o'clock at night they beat up the drums and sounded the calls and called out the guard and the guard calls us all out, and the road is red and slippery, and every soldier in the camp no longer in the camp but in the streets of the city, rifle-butts, bayonets, every street cut off for eight blocks north and west the opera-house. And that's how it began.

HURST (*the frenzy rising*): The streets is empty, but the houses is full. He says, 'no undue measures, minimum violence', he says. 'But bring in the killers.'

ATTERCLIFFE: The killers are gone, they've gone miles off in that time—sporting away, right up in the mountains, I told you at the time.

MUSGRAVE: That's not material, there's one man is dead, but there's everyone's responsible.

HURST: So bring the lot in! It's easy, they're all in bed, kick the front doors down, knock 'em on the head, boys, chuck 'em in the wagons.

ATTERCLIFFE: I didn't know she was only a little kid, there was scores of 'em on that staircase, pitch-dark, trampling, screaming, they're all of 'em screaming, what are we to do?

HURST: Knock 'em on the head, boys, chuck 'em in the wagons.

ATTERCLIFFE: How was I to tell she was only a little kid?

MUSGRAVE (*bringing it to an end*): THAT'S NOT MATERIAL! You were told to bring 'em in. If you killed her, you killed her! She was just one, and who cares a damn for that! Stay in your place and keep your hands on that Gatling. We've got to have order here, whatever there was there; and I can tell you it wasn't order. . . . (*To Hurst*) You, take a rifle. Leave your drum down.
(*Hurst jumps up on the plinth, takes a rifle and loads.*)
We've got to have order. So I'll just tell you quietly how many there were was put down as injured—that's badly hurt, hospital, we don't count knocks and bruises, any o' that. Twenty-five men. Nine women. No children, whatever he says. She was a fully grown girl, and she had a known record as an associate of terrorists. That was her. Then four men, one of them elderly, turned out to have died too. Making five. Not so very many. Dark streets. Natural surge of rage.
HURST: We didn't find the killers.
MUSGRAVE: Of course we didn't find 'em. Not then we didn't, any road. We didn't even know 'em. But I know 'em, now. One man, and for him five. Therefore, for five of them we multiply out, and we find it five-and-twenty. . . . So, as I understand Logic and Logic to me is the mechanism of God—that means that today there's twenty-five persons will have to be——

JOHN ARDEN

Questions

1 What do we know about the soldier whose skeleton was shown? How had he been killed? What was he doing at the time?

2 Was the soldier in any way to blame for his own death?

3 Where had the regiment been stationed when the soldier was killed?

4 Why had the troops been particularly angry about this murder?

5 What orders did the troops have when turned out after the murder?

6 What is Attercliffe's objection to the search for the killers? Why does Musgrave say this objection is 'not material' (l. 36)?

7 What was the casualty figure among civilians that night?

8 What was achieved by the search?

9 Can you supply the final word that Musgrave fails to give? What is the penalty he demands of his hearers?

10 By what logic does he justify this demanded penalty?

Implications

11 What value do you attach to the order 'no undue measures, minimum violence'?

12 If there was little chance of catching the killers, why were troops ordered out to search the town?

13 Musgrave says 'I know 'em, now' (l. 63). Who in his opinion were responsible for all this killing?

14 If Musgrave had gone on to kill twenty-five townspeople, would that have concluded the matter of the soldier's death?

15 What is meant by 'collective punishment'? What examples of it can you give? How effective is it?

16 Would you say that Musgrave was patriotic?

Exercises

17 Describe an occasion when you were an innocent victim.

18 Write a story entitled 'Pointless Revenge'.

19 Write a newspaper article, with headline, covering the events of the night on which the soldier was shot.

¶ *Many people wish to be just ordinary and safe. Is this a worthy ambition?*

¶ *Are there today any causes worth risking comfort and security for?*

Each His Own Wilderness

[In this play, a young man, Tony, has just learnt that his mother, Myra, has sold the house in which they both live. Rosemary, a girl of about Tony's age, tries to keep the peace between them.]

TONY: My God, my mother's done that to me. She's done that to me. She's my mother and she might just as well have taken a knife and stabbed me with it. She's my mother and she knows so little about me that she doesn't suspect that there's one thing I love in this world, and it's this house. Now we'll have to leave here and live in some—damned pretty little flat somewhere. I can't bear it, I can't bear it. . . . (*There is a silence. Myra slowly straightens herself, stands up, walks slowly across the room. Rosemary watches her fearfully.*)

MYRA: If you hate me as much as that why do you put so much energy into getting me alone with you into this house? Well, why? For the pleasure of torturing me? Or of being tortured?

ROSEMARY: Oh, Myra, he didn't mean it.

MYRA (*with a short laugh*): Perhaps he does mean it. There's no law that says a son must like his mother, is there? (*after a pause*) And vice versa. (*She lights a cigarette. It can be seen that her hand is trembling violently. Otherwise she is calm. Almost limp, with the same limpness as Tony's.*)

TONY (*looking at her, he begins to understand what he has done. Almost apologetically*): I can't think why one of you doesn't say: There are millions of people in the world living in mud huts, and you make this fuss about moving from one comfortable home to another. Isn't that what I'm supposed to be feeling?

MYRA: Since you've said it, there's no need for me to.

TONY (*almost querulous*): The other thing you could say is: Wait until you've got to my age and see if you've done any better. Well—if I haven't done any better I'd have the grace to kill myself.

MYRA: Luckily I don't take myself so seriously. Well, I'm going to leave you to it.

TONY (*desperately anxious*): What do you mean, where are you going?

MYRA: I don't know.

TONY: You're not going?

MYRA: Why not? I don't propose to live with someone who can't stand me. Why should I. . . . (*She makes a movement as if expanding, or about to take flight.*) It just occurs to me that for the first time in my life I'm free.

TONY: Mother, where are you going?

MYRA: It occurs to me that for the last twenty-two years my life has been governed by yours—by your needs. Oh, you may not think so—but the way I've lived, what I've done, my whole life has been governed by your needs. And what for . . . (*contemptuously*). What for—a little monster of egotism—that's what you are. A petty, envious, spiteful little egotist, concerned with nothing but yourself.

ROSEMARY (*almost in tears*): Oh Myra, stop, stop.

MYRA (*ignoring her, to Tony*): Well, I'm sure it's my fault. Obviously it is. If I've spent half my life bringing you up and you turn out—as you have—then it's my life that's a failure, isn't it? Well, it's not going to be a failure in future.

TONY: Mother, what are you going to do?

MYRA: There are a lot of things I've wanted to do for a long time, and I haven't done them. (*Laughing*) Perhaps I'll take the money and go off; why not? Or perhaps I'll be a tramp. I could be, you know. I could walk out of this house with my needs in a small suitcase . . . and I shall. Or perhaps I'll go on that boat to the Pacific to the testing area—I wanted to do that and didn't, because of you.

TONY: Mother, you might get killed.

MYRA: Dear me, I might get killed. And what of it? I don't propose to keep my life clutched in my hand like small change. . . .

TONY: Mother, you can't just walk off into—nothing.

MYRA: Nothing? I don't have to shelter under a heap of old bricks—like a frightened mouse. I'm going. I'll come back and collect what I need when I've decided what I'm going to do (*goes towards door*).

TONY (*angry and frightened*): Mother.

(*She turns at the door. She is quite calm, but she is crying.*)

Mother, you're crying.

MYRA (*laughing*): Why not? I'm nearly fifty—and it's true there's nothing much to show for it. Except that I've never been afraid to take chances and make mistakes. I've never wanted security and safety and the walls of respectability—you damned little petty bourgeois. My God, the irony of it—that we should have given birth to a generation of little office boys and clerks and . . . little people who count their pensions before they're out of school . . . little petty bourgeois. Yes, I am crying. I've been alive for fifty years. Isn't that good enough cause for tears . . . (*she goes out*).

TONY (*amazed, not believing it*): But Rosemary, she's gone.

ROSEMARY: Yes.

TONY: But she'll come back.

ROSEMARY: No, I don't think so. (*She comes to him, puts her arm around him. They crouch down, side by side, arms around each other.*)

TONY: Rosemary, do you know that not one word of what she said made any sense to me at all . . . slogans, slogans, slogans. . . ?

ROSEMARY: What's the matter with being safe—and ordinary? What's wrong with being ordinary—and safe?

TONY: Rosemary, listen—never in the whole history of the world have people made a battle-cry out of being ordinary. Never. Supposing we all said to the politicians—we refuse to be heroic. We refuse to be brave. We are bored with all the noble gestures —what then, Rosemary?

ROSEMARY: Yes. Ordinary and safe.

TONY: Leave us alone, we'll say. Leave us alone to live. Just leave us alone. . . .

DORIS LESSING

Questions

1 Why is Tony so furious with his mother for selling the house?

2 How do we know in the speech about the mud huts that Tony has correctly voiced his mother's feelings?

3 Why does Myra feel freed?

4 Whom does Myra blame for her son's selfishness?

5 What does Myra mean by saying she will 'go on that boat to the Pacific to the testing area' (l. 55)?

6 Whom does Myra mean by 'we' in saying 'the irony of it—that we should have given birth to . . .' (l. 73)?

7 What does she mean by 'petty bourgeois' (l. 73)?

8 'Slogans' (l. 85). Which of Myra's remarks might Tony most justly have called slogans?

9 'Noble gestures' (l. 91). What has Tony in mind?

10 Tony thinks his mother's life has been a mess, a failure. Where can we see this most clearly from what he says?

Implications

11 Why does Myra think her son petty? Why does Tony think his mother a failure? How far do you agree with either of them, from what you can tell in this scene?

12 Is there anything wrong with wanting to be ordinary and safe?

13 What opportunities has anyone today of being brave and heroic?

14 What did Myra mean by counting pensions before being out of school?

15 What is Myra's defiant boast? Is it worth being proud of?

Exercises

16 In a paragraph sum up all that Myra accuses her son of. In another paragraph sum up all that Tony accuses her of.

17 Put yourself in Myra's place and write down how you might use £500. Then put yourself in Tony's place and do the same for him.

18 Write an account of what you would like to have achieved by the time you are Myra's age—fifty.

Discussion and Writing

Photograph No. 9 (facing page 114)

Why are these people on the road?

What sort of people are they? What moods do they appear to be in?

Should they be permitted to make their opinions felt in this way? What other ways have they? Are the other ways as effective?

Is the picture representative of what demonstrations now look like in this country?

As a witness of this part of the procession, write an account of the people you have seen in it, of their appearance and their behaviour.

Write the words of a marching song for these demonstrators.

10 Toleration

¶ Is there any justification for segregation of schools by colour?

¶ What objections, if any, would you have to working alongside someone of a different colour?

¶ How would you answer someone who criticised you for having people of a different colour into your home?

The Black Madonna

A dozen Jamaicans were taken on at the motor works. Two came into Raymond's department. He invited them to the flat one evening to have coffee. They were unmarried, very polite and black. The quiet one was called Henry Pierce and the talkative one, Oxford St John. Lou, to Raymond's surprise and pleasure, decided that all their acquaintances, from top to bottom, must meet Henry and Oxford. All along he hàd known she was not a snob, only sensible, but he had rather feared she would consider the mixing of their new black and their old white friends not sensible.

'I'm glad you like Henry and Oxford,' he said. 'I'm glad we're able to introduce them to so many people.' For the dark pair had, within a month, spent nine evenings at Cripps House; they had met accountants, teachers, packers, and sorters. Only Tina Farrell, the usherette, had not seemed to understand the quality of these occasions: 'Quite nice chaps, them darkies, when you get to know them.'

'You mean Jamaicans,' said Lou. 'Why shouldn't they be nice? They're no different from anyone else.'

'Yes, yes, that's what I mean,' said Tina.

'We're all equal,' stated Lou. 'Don't forget there are black Bishops.'

'Jesus, I never said we were the equal of a Bishop,' Tina said, very bewildered.

'Well, don't call them darkies.'

Sometimes, on summer Sunday afternoons Raymond and Lou took their friends for a run in their car, ending up at a riverside road-house. The first time they turned up with Oxford and Henry they felt defiant; but there were no objections, there was no trouble at all. Soon the dark pair ceased to be a novelty. Oxford St John took up with a pretty red-haired book-keeper, and Henry Pierce, missing his companion, spent more of his time at the Parkers' flat. Lou and Raymond had planned to spend their two weeks' summer holiday in London. 'Poor Henry,' said Lou. 'He'll miss us.'

Once you brought him out he was not so quiet as you thought at first. Henry was twenty-four, desirous of knowledge in all fields, shining very much in eyes, skin, teeth, which made him seem all the more eager. He called out the maternal in Lou, and to some extent the avuncular in Raymond. Lou used to love him when he read out lines from his favourite poems which he had copied into an exercise book.

> Haste thee, nymph, and bring with thee
> Jest and youthful jollity,
> Sport that . . .

Lou would interrupt: 'You should say jest, jollity—not yest, yollity.'

'Jest,' he said carefully. 'And laughter holding both his sides,' he continued. 'Laughter—hear that, Lou?—laughter. That's what the human race was made for. Those folks that go round gloomy, Lou, they . . .'

Lou loved this talk. Raymond puffed his pipe benignly.

* * *

'He'll miss us when we go on our holidays.'

Raymond telephoned to the hotel in London. 'Have you a single room for a young gentleman accompanying Mr and Mrs Parker?' He added, 'a coloured gentleman'. To his pleasure a room was available, and to his relief there was no objection to Henry's colour.

They enjoyed their London holiday, but it was somewhat marred by a visit to that widowed sister of Lou's to whom she allowed a pound a week towards the rearing of her eight children. Lou had not seen her sister Elizabeth for nine years.

They went to her one day towards the end of their holiday. Henry sat at the back of the car beside a large suitcase stuffed with old clothes for Elizabeth. Raymond at the wheel kept saying, 'Poor Elizabeth—eight kids,' which irritated Lou, though she kept her peace.

On the way back to the hotel Lou chattered with relief that it was over. 'Poor Elizabeth, she hasn't had much of a chance. I liked little Francis, what did you think of little Francis, Ray?'

THE WORLD COMMUNITY

Raymond did not like being called Ray, but he made no objection for he knew that Lou had been under a long strain. Elizabeth had not been very pleasant. She had expressed admiration for Lou's hat, bag, gloves, and shoes which were all navy blue, but she had used an accusing tone. The house had been smelly and dirty. 'I'll show you round,' Elizabeth had said in a tone of mock refinement, and they were forced to push through a dark narrow passage behind her skinny form till they came to the big room where the children slept. A row of old iron beds each with a tumble of dark blanket rugs, no sheets. Raymond was indignant at the sight and hoped that Lou was not feeling upset. He knew very well Elizabeth had a decent living income from a number of public sources, and was simply a slut, one of those who would not help themselves.

Lou's chatter on the way back to the hotel had a touch of hysteria. 'Raymond, dear,' she said in her most chirpy West End voice, 'I simply had to give the poor dear all my next week's housekeeping money. We shall have to starve, darling, when we get home. That's simply what we shall have to do.'

'O.K.,' said Raymond.

'I ask you,' Lou shrieked, 'what else could I do, what could I do?'

'Nothing at all,' said Raymond, 'but what you've done.'

'My own sister, my dear,' said Lou; 'and did you see the way she had her hair bleached?—All streaky, and she used to have a lovely head of hair.'

'I wonder if she tries to raise herself?' said Raymond.

'With all those children she could surely get better accommodation if only she——'

'That sort,' said Henry, leaning forward from the back of the car, 'never moves. It's the slum mentality, man. Take some folks I've seen back home——'

'There's no comparison,' Lou snapped suddenly, 'this is quite a different case.'

Raymond glanced at her in surprise: Henry sat back, offended. Lou was thinking wildly, what a cheek *him* talking like a snob. At least Elizabeth's white.

MURIEL SPARK

(This story is one of a collection entitled *The Go-Away Bird*.)

Questions

1 Why was Raymond surprised and pleased when his wife decided that all their friends must meet Henry and Oxford?

TOLERATION

2   Why did Lou correct Tina Farrell?

3   Why did Raymond and Lou feel defiant when they first took their friends to the road-house?

4 *a*   How would you describe Raymond's and Lou's attitudes towards Henry?

b   How does the author describe their feelings towards him?

5   Why did Raymond and Lou decide to take Henry on holiday with them?

6   What was the purpose of their visit to Lou's sister?

7   When Raymond saw the state of Elizabeth's flat and family he 'was indignant at the sight' (l. 79). Why?

8   What upset Lou about her sister? How does Lou show her distress?

9   Why does Lou say she simply *had* to give Elizabeth all her housekeeping money? Could she have done anything else?

10   Lou thought 'what a cheek *him* talking like a snob' (l. 103). Why was she so indignant with Henry?

Implications

11   Were Raymond and Lou wise to try and befriend Oxford and Henry? What were their motives?

12   Was Henry being unfair in his comment 'It's the slum mentality' (l. 98)? What does he mean by this? Was this 'talking like a snob' as Lou thinks?

13   What do we learn about Lou from her unuttered remark 'At least Elizabeth's white' (l. 103)?

14   Lou objects to Tina calling the Jamaicans 'darkies' (l. 15). Why?

15   'They're no different from anyone else' (l. 18). Are people all alike?

Exercises

16   Put yourself in Henry's place and write his description of Elizabeth's flat.

17   Write about any person of your own age whom you know but who differs from you in colour. Say honestly in what ways you differ and in what ways are similar.

18   Write a letter to your M.P. objecting to an instance of colour prejudice that you know of.

¶ *If hundreds of hungry immigrants or refugees started to arrive in your home district, how would it affect local life?*

¶ *Should a full chance of employment be given to English-speaking immigrants arriving in your district?*

¶ *Do you feel you should be free to look for work and a bonus in any part of your own country?*

The Grapes of Wrath

[Not long ago in the United States, a whole section of the population of Oklahoma was driven to migrate west to California. They were not welcome. They looked like the family in Photograph 2, page 19.]

The moving, questing people were migrants now. Those families which had lived on a little piece of land, who had lived and died on forty acres, had eaten or starved on the products of forty acres, had now the whole West to rove in. And they scampered about, looking for work; and the highways were streams of people, and the ditch banks were lines of people. Behind them more were coming. The great highways streamed with moving people. There in the Middle- and South-West had lived a simple agrarian folk who had not changed with industry, who had not formed with machines or known the power and danger of machines in private hands. They had not grown up in the paradoxes of industry. Their senses were still sharp to the ridiculousness of the industrial life.

And then suddenly the machines pushed them out and they swarmed on the highways. The movement changed them; the highways, the camps along the road, the fear of hunger and the hunger itself, changed them. The children without dinner changed them, the endless moving changed them. They were migrants. And the hostility changed them, welded them, united them—hostility that made the little towns group and arm as though to repel an invader, squads with pick-handles, clerks and storekeepers with shotguns, guarding the world against their own people.

In the West there was panic when the migrants multiplied on the highways. Men of property were terrified for their property. Men who had never been hungry saw the eyes of the hungry. Men who had never wanted anything very much saw the flare of want in the eyes of the migrants. And the men of the towns and of the soft

PEACE COMMITTE
OF THE
SOCIETY OF FRIENDS
(QUAKERS)
SOLD BY
BAN THE BOMB

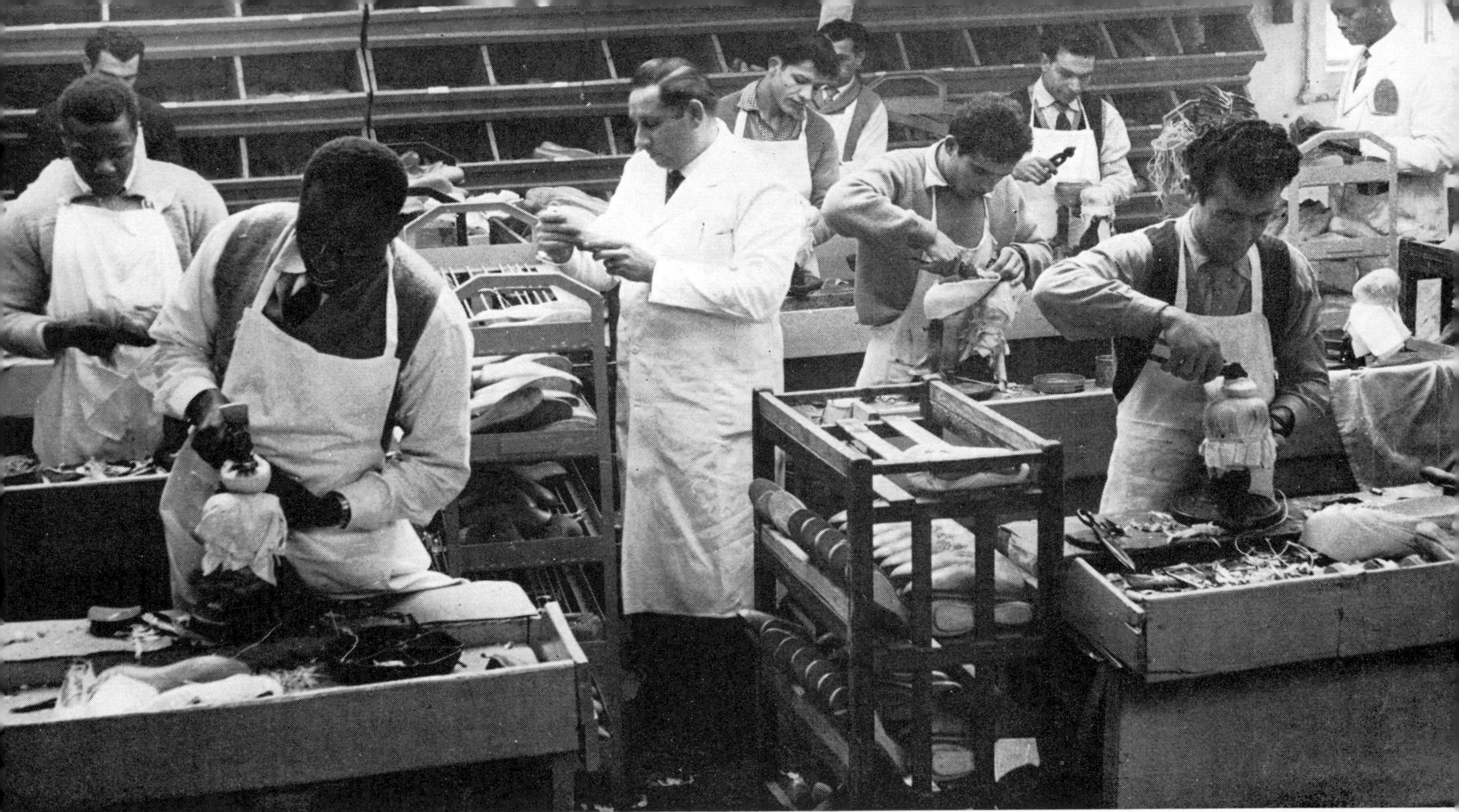

suburban country gathered to defend themselves; and they reassured themselves that they were good and the invaders bad, as a man must do before he fights. They said: These goddamned Okies are dirty and ignorant. They're degenerate, sexual maniacs. These goddamned Okies are thieves. They'll steal anything. They've got no sense of property rights.

And the latter was true, for how can a man without property know the ache of ownership? And the defending people said: They bring disease, they're filthy. We can't have them in the schools. They're strangers. How'd you like to have your sister go out with one of 'em?

The local people whipped themselves into a mould of cruelty. Then they formed units, squads, and armed them—armed them with clubs, with gas, with guns. We own the country. We can't let these Okies get out of hand. And the men who were armed did not own the land, but they thought they did. And the clerks who drilled at night owned nothing, and the little storekeepers possessed only a drawerful of debts. But even a debt is something, even a job is something. The clerk thought: I get fifteen dollars a week. S'pose a goddam Okie would work for twelve? And the little storekeeper thought: How could I compete with a debtless man?

And the migrants streamed in on the highways and their hunger was in their eyes, and their need was in their eyes. They had no argument, no system, nothing but their numbers and their needs. When there was work for a man, ten men fought for it—fought with a low wage. If that fella'll work for thirty cents, I'll work for twenty-five.

If he'll take twenty-five, I'll do it for twenty.

No, me, I'm hungry. I'll work for fifteen. I'll work for food. The kids. You ought to see them. Little boils, like, comin' out, an' they can't run aroun'. Give 'em some windfall fruit, an' they bloated up. Me, I'll work for a little piece of meat.

And this was good, for wages went down and prices stayed up. The great owners were glad and they sent out more handbills to bring more people in. And wages went down and prices stayed up. And pretty soon now we'll have serfs again.

And now the great owners and the companies invented a new method. A great owner bought a cannery. And when the peaches and the pears were ripe he cut the price of fruit below the cost of raising it. And as cannery owner he paid himself a low price for the fruit and kept the price of canned goods up and took his profit. And the little farmers who owned no canneries lost their farms, and they were taken by the great owners, the banks, and the companies who also owned the canneries. As time went on, there were fewer farms. The little farmers moved into town for a while and exhausted their credit, exhausted their friends, their relatives. And then they, too, went on the highways. And the roads were crowded with men ravenous for work, murderous for work.

And the companies, the banks worked at their own doom and they did not know it. The fields were fruitful, and starving men moved on the roads. The granaries were full and the children of the poor grew up rachitic, and the pustules of pellagra swelled on their sides. The great companies did not know that the line between hunger and anger is a thin line. And money that might have gone to wages went for gas, for guns, for agents and spies, for blacklists, for drilling. On the highways the people moved like ants and searched for work, for food. And the anger began to ferment.

JOHN STEINBECK

Questions

1 What indicates in the first paragraph that the migrants would find town life strange?

2 What frightened the people of the West about the migrants?

3 How did the Westerners reassure themselves 'that they were good and the invaders bad' (l. 28)?

4 What is meant by 'guarding the world against their own people' (l. 21)?

5 What exactly did the Westerners fear if the Okies should 'get out of hand'? What did they fear losing?

6 Why would a migrant man work for so low a wage?

7 '... soon now we'll have serfs again' (l. 62). What were serfs? What does the sentence mean?

8 What was the effect on the small farmer of the big companies using cheap labour to grow rich?

9 What does the author mean by 'the line between hunger and anger is a thin line' (l. 79)?

10 Steinbeck twice mentions 'gas and guns' (l. 40 and l. 81). Who bought them? Why? How were they paid for?

Implications

11 Might the migrants have had good reason to be diseased, dirty and ignorant?

12 Is there a contradiction between calling them ignorant and yet saying 'we can't have them in our schools'?

13 These arguments were used by white Americans about white Americans. Where might one hear any of the same arguments being used today? Have you heard any of them? About whom? Were they justified?

14 Should a man steal if his family is starving?

15 What could these Westerners have done in a positive way to accommodate the migrants?

16 What groups of people in England might be accused of being dirty, ignorant, diseased and immoral? How justified is the accusation? What can we do about it?

Exercises

17 Recount in your own words the way in which a Western farmer might become a vagrant.

18 Write a dialogue between a Westerner and an Okie who is looking for work.

19 Make a list of practical, helpful 'Do's and don'ts' for newcomers from abroad in your area.

20 Write a letter to the Home Secretary suggesting ways in which newcomers to Britain could be helped settle here.

¶ *In a free country should one be free to express any opinions one holds? Is there anyone to whom you would not apply this?*

¶ *Think of the person whose views on politics or religion you most strongly disagree with. Would you have that person's opinions silenced? How could they be silenced?*

The Power and the Glory

[In 1938 the Mexican government suppressed the church and persecuted the priests, hunting them down and shooting them: no one was allowed to attend a religious service. Here the last priest left in the state, disguised as a peasant, is caught in a police search at the village where he has just held Mass.]

The lieutenant said, 'Search the huts.' Time passed very slowly: even the smoke of the shot seemed to remain in the air for an unnatural period. Some pigs came grunting out of a hut, and a turkey-cock paced with evil dignity into the centre of the circle, puffing out its dusty feathers and tossing the long pink membrane from its beak. A soldier came up to the lieutenant and saluted sketchily. He said, 'They're all here.'

'You've found nothing suspicious?'

'No.'

'Then look again.'

Once more time stopped like a broken clock. The lieutenant drew out a cigarette-case, hesitated and put it back again. Again the policeman approached and reported, 'Nothing.'

The lieutenant barked out, 'Attention. All of you. Listen to me.' The outer ring of police closed in, pushing the villagers together into a small group in front of the lieutenant: only the children were left free. The priest saw his own child standing close to the lieutenant's horse: she could just reach above his boot: she put up her hand and touched the leather. The lieutenant said, 'I am looking for two men —one is a gringo, a yankee, a murderer. I can see very well he is not here. There is a reward of five hundred pesos for his capture. Keep your eyes open.' He paused and ran his eye over them: the priest felt his gaze come to rest; he looked down like the others at the ground.

'The other,' the lieutenant said, 'is a priest.' He raised his voice: 'You know what this means—traitor to the republic. Anyone who shelters him is a traitor too.' Their immobility seemed to anger him. He said, 'You're fools if you still believe what the priests tell you. All they want is your money. What has God ever done for you? Have you got enough to eat? Have your children got enough to eat? Instead of food they talk to you about heaven. Oh, everything will be fine after you are dead, they say. I tell you—everything will be fine when they are dead, and you must help.' The child had her hand on his boot. He looked down at her with dark affection. He said with conviction, 'This child is worth more than the Pope in Rome.' The police leant on their guns: one of them yawned—the turkey-cock went hissing back towards the hut. The lieutenant said, 'If you've seen this priest speak up. There is a reward of seven hundred pesos. . . .' Nobody spoke.

The lieutenant yanked his horse's head round towards them; he said, 'We know he's in this district. Perhaps you don't know what happened to a man in Concepción.' One of the women began to weep. He said, 'Come up—one after the other—and let me have your names. No, not the women, the men.'

They filed sullenly up and he questioned them, 'What's your name? What do you do? Married? Which is your wife? Have you heard of this priest?' Only one man now stood between the priest and the horse's head. He recited an act of contrition silently with only half a mind—'. . . my sins, because they have crucified my loving Saviour . . . but above all because they have offended. . . .' He was alone in front of the lieutenant—'I hereby resolve never more to offend Thee. . . .' It was a formal act, because a man had to be prepared: it was like making your will—and might be as valueless.

'Your name?'

The name of the man in Concepción came back to him. He said, 'Montez.'

'Have you ever seen the priest?'

'No.'

'What do you do?'

'I have a little land.'

'Are you married?'

'Yes.'

'Which is your wife?'

Maria suddenly broke out: 'It's me. Why do you want to ask so many questions? Do you think he looks like a priest?'

The lieutenant was examining something on the pommel of his saddle: it seemed to be an old photograph. 'Let me see your hands,' he said.

The priest held them up: they were as hard as a labourer's. Suddenly the lieutenant leant down from the saddle and sniffed at his breath. There was complete silence among the villagers—a dangerous silence, because it seemed to convey to the lieutenant a fear. . . . He stared back at the hollow stubbled face, looked back at the photograph. 'All right,' he said, 'next.'

The last man gave his evidence.

The lieutenant said, 'Is no one willing to help?'

They stood silent beside the decayed bandstand. He said, 'You heard what happened at Concepción. I took a hostage there . . . and when I found that this priest had been in the neighbourhood I put

80 the man against the nearest tree. I found out because there's always somebody who changes his mind—perhaps because somebody in Concepción loved the man's wife and wanted him out of the way. It's not my business to look into reasons. I only know we found wine later in Concepción. . . . Perhaps there's somebody in this village who wants your piece of land—or your cow. It's much safer to speak now. Because I'm going to take a hostage from here too.' He paused. Then he said, 'There's no need even to speak, if he's here among you. Just look at him. No one will know then that it was you who gave him away. He won't know himself if you're
90 afraid of his curses. Now . . . this is your last chance.'

The priest looked at the ground—he wasn't going to make it difficult for the man who gave him away.

'Right,' the lieutenant said, 'then I shall choose my man. You've brought it on yourselves.'

GRAHAM GREENE

Questions

1 Who were the police searching for?

2 Give at least two of the lieutenant's accusations against the priests.

3 Who was 'the man in Concepción'? What had happened to him?

4 How can we tell that the priest is afraid? Is this the same as being cowardly?

5 How does Maria protect the priest?

6 Why does the lieutenant examine the priest's hands? Why does he smell his breath?

7 How else does the lieutenant hope to identify the priest?

8 What had the police found when searching in Concepción? What was the significance of their find?

9 How could the villagers most easily have indicated the priest to the lieutenant?

10 Why, at the end, is the lieutenant going to choose a man?

Implications

11 What can we gather about the living conditions of these villagers?

12 What attitude do the lieutenant's men seem to be showing towards the villagers?
13 What does the lieutenant blame the priests for?
14 What does the lieutenant say he is trying to do for the peasants?
15 Does the banning of the priests and services seem to have affected the villagers' attitude towards the police?
16 Why might anyone in the village have been tempted to betray the priest?
17 Should people be permitted to follow whatever form of religion they wish to? Are there any forms of religion that we could not tolerate in Britain? Does the same go for political belief?
18 What, if anything, can we not afford to tolerate?

Exercises

19 Write out the lieutenant's official report on the search in this village.
20 In your own words report what the lieutenant said to the assembled villagers.
21 Write a dialogue between two villagers after the event—one in favour of betraying the priest, the other in favour of concealing him.
22 Write an imaginary account of a search in your own home district for a suspect whom your friends are concealing.

Discussion and Writing

Photograph No. 10 (facing page 45)

In terms of race and colour, how would you describe each of the men in this shop?

How are the two checkers distinguished from the other men?

What is your own reaction to the possibility of working under the supervision of someone from a race different to your own?

The factory shown in the photograph employs thirteen different nationalities. Write your views on how you would like to work there.

11 International Relations

¶ *What differences in habit have you noticed among people from other parts of Britain? Which of their habits annoy you?*

¶ *What characteristics of foreigners have amused or annoyed you? Which of your own characteristics do you think might amuse or surprise a foreigner?*

A Pattern of Islands

Walking down the bright avenue, the white man had no need to pry if he wanted to see the villagers at home. The people did not use their screens to shut out friendly eyes or conversation. Men back from fishing or cultivation loved to loll at ease on their floors, smoking and bandying talk from house to house. Women and girls sat brushing their hair, braiding flower-chains, changing garments, bathing children, plaiting mats, chattering all the time, but alive to the littlest thing that passed in the village street. If you wanted a silent and reflective stroll, you avoided a village, for it was almost beyond human power to resist the temptation of their charming and curious gossip. Everything was news for the villagers, especially the women.

You might contrive to avoid sitting or standing talk, but there was always that bare minimum of conversation you must give to everyone who greeted you. The form of exchange never varied:

VILLAGER: Sir, thou shalt be blest. Whence comest thou?
SELF: Sir (or Woman), thou shalt be blest. I come from the south.
VILLAGER: Aia! And whither goest thou?
SELF: I go northwards.
VILLAGER: Aia! And what to do in the north?
SELF: Just to walk.
VILLAGER: Ai-i-ia! We shall meet again.
SELF: We shall meet again.
VILLAGER: So good-bye.
SELF: Good-bye.

And if you met the same person again on your way back, which was most probable at the idle hour of the sundown stroll:

VILLAGER: Sir, thou shalt be blest. Art thou back?
SELF: Sir, thou shalt be blest. I am back.

VILLAGER: And whither now?
SELF: I go to my house.
VILLAGER: To do what in thy house?
SELF: Just to sit down.
VILLAGER: Ai-i-ia! We shall meet again.
SELF: We shall meet again.
VILLAGER: So good-bye.
SELF: Good-bye.

I ventured once in the very early days to tell the Old Man that I found these exchanges a little redundant. He bent his thin dark look on me: 'You probably think, Grimble, that you're here to teach these people our code of manners, not to learn theirs. You're making a big mistake.'

He only gave one of his curiously narrow-nosed double-barrelled sniffs at my denial, and continued: 'Well . . . I'll tell you something that happened to me not long ago. I carpeted the Tabiang *Kaubure* (village headman) the other day to complain to him about the old men's habit of hawking and spitting when they get excited in the Native Court. I told him he must talk to them about it. My grievance was that a sudden outburst of that kind had drowned my voice when I was speaking to them. . . .'

'If I had put the thing to him as an offence against hygiene,' he continued, 'the Kaubure would have got on their tails at once, but I didn't. All I talked to him about was the breach of courtesy to me. And this is what he did. He came forward to my desk and laid his hands on mine. Then he looked me straight in the eyes and said, "How can I speak for you to the old men of Tabiang when you did what you did there only yesterday? Even you, who hold us in the palm of your hand?"'

It appeared that, in walking through Tabiang the day before, he had passed between two women—the wife and daughter of an elder —as they were chatting to each other across the road. Seeing them in conversation, he should have stopped before crossing their line of vision and asked permission to go on. There was a proper formula of words for that: 'E matauninga te aba? (Are the people offended?)' Had he used it, he would have been assured at once that nobody could be the least bit offended. But even then, it would have been proper for him to pass forward with head and shoulders bowed well below their eye-line. His omission of these formalities had been the more astounding to the people because of his exalted rank among them. They had a proverb, 'Small is the voice of a chief', which meant, in general, that gentleness and courtesy should walk hand in hand with power.

'The Kaubure told me all this so quietly,' went on the Old Man, 'that I felt a fearful bounder. Of course, I asked him to take my apologies to Tabiang, and all was well again. But it was lucky for me he had the guts to talk as he did. Sometimes they don't talk, but keep it bottled up, and then things happen, and they get the blame in the long run when the initial fault was really ours. You may walk round the villages satisfied you're a hell of a fellow, while all the time they're thinking what a mannerless young pup you are... yes, and forgiving you too, and staying loyal in spite of everything. Let that sink in, and go and learn a bit about them. Yours is the honour, not theirs.'

SIR ARTHUR GRIMBLE

[Sir Arthur Grimble was for many years with the Colonial Service in the Gilbert and Ellice Islands in the Western Pacific. The Old Man referred to here is Grimble's senior, the Resident Commissioner, and at the time the author was a cadet District Officer.]

Questions

1 Why was it impossible to walk through the village without exchanging greetings?

2 What does the word 'redundant' mean here (l. 39)? What did Grimble mean by saying he found 'these exchanges a little redundant'?

3 What is the meaning of 'a code of manners' (l. 41)?

4 'You're making a big mistake', the Old Man says to Grimble. What was this mistake?

5 What had the Old Man complained of to the kaubure?

6 Why did the Old Man not try to explain his ideas about hygiene to the kaubure?

7 What had the Old Man's offence been?

8 What had made this offence seem even worse when committed by a Resident Commissioner?

9 What was the Old Man's reaction to the kaubure's criticism?

10 'Yours is the honour, not theirs.' How do you explain the Old Man's final remark?

Implications

11   What do you think gave the Kaubure the confidence to speak openly to the Old Man like that?

12   Who had been the more ill-mannered, the old men in the court, or the Old Man?

13   What do you think would have resulted from trying to make the islanders do things in European style?

Exercises

14   Imagine you are one of the villagers who saw the Resident Commissioner commit his mistake. Write down what you might have said in reporting it to your Kaubure.

15   Write out the conventional greetings exchanged upon meeting by the following pairs:
 a   you and a friend;
 b   you and an older neighbour;
 c   you and a stranger whose town or village you are visiting.

16   Write the entry that Grimble might have made in his diary after this interview with his superior.

¶ *Have you ever been amused watching someone in authority caught in a difficult situation? What did they do and was this what you had expected?*

¶ *How could you best get to know a foreigner? By having one to live in your home? By working for one? By going abroad in the Forces?*

Shooting an Elephant

The orderly came back in a few minutes with a rifle and five cartridges, and meanwhile some Burmans had arrived and told us that the elephant was in the paddy fields below, only a few hundred yards away. As I started forward practically the whole population of the quarter flocked out of the houses and followed me. They had seen the rifle and were all shouting excitedly that I was going to shoot the elephant. They had not shown much interest in the elephant when he was merely ravaging their homes, but it was different now that he was going to be shot. It was a bit of fun to them, as it would be to an English crowd; besides they wanted the meat. It made me vaguely uneasy. I had no intention of shooting the elephant—I had merely sent for the rifle to defend myself if necessary—and it is always unnerving to have a crowd following you. I marched down the hill, looking and feeling a fool, with the rifle over my shoulder and an ever-growing army of people jostling at my heels. At the bottom, when you got away from the huts, there was a metalled road and beyond that a miry waste of paddy fields a thousand yards across, not yet ploughed but soggy from the first rains and dotted with coarse grass. The elephant was standing eight yards from the road, his left side towards us. He took not the slightest notice of the crowd's approach. He was tearing up bunches of grass, beating them against his knees to clean them and stuffing them into his mouth.

I had halted on the road. As soon as I saw the elephant I knew with perfect certainty that I ought not to shoot him. It is a serious matter to shoot a working elephant—it is comparable to destroying a huge and costly piece of machinery—and obviously one ought not to do it if it can possibly be avoided. And at that distance, peacefully eating, the elephant looked no more dangerous than a cow. I thought then and I think now that this attack of 'must' was already passing off; in which case he would merely wander harmlessly about until the mahout came back and caught him. Moreover, I did not in the least want to shoot him. I decided that I would watch him for a little while to make sure that he did not turn savage again, and then go home.

But at that moment I glanced round at the crowd that had followed me. It was an immense crowd, two thousand at the least and growing every minute. It blocked the road for a long distance on either side. I looked at the sea of yellow faces above the garish clothes—faces all happy and excited over this bit of fun, all certain that the elephant was going to be shot. They were watching me as they would watch a conjurer about to perform a trick. They did not like me, but with the magical rifle in my hands I was momentarily worth watching. And suddenly I realised that I should have to shoot the elephant after all. The people expected it of me and I had got to do it; I could feel their two thousand wills pressing me forward, irresistibly. And it was at this moment, as I stood there with the rifle in my hands, that I first grasped the hollowness, the futility of the white man's dominion in the East. Here was I, the white man with his gun, standing in front of the unarmed native crowd— seemingly the leading actor of the piece; but in reality I was only an absurd puppet pushed to and fro by the will of those yellow faces behind. I perceived in this moment that when the white man turns tyrant it is his own freedom that he destroys. He becomes a sort of hollow, posing dummy, the conventional figure of a sahib. For it is the condition of his rule that he shall spend his life in trying to impress the 'natives' and so in every crisis he has got to do what the 'natives' expect of him. He wears a mask, and his face grows to fit it. I had got to shoot the elephant. I had committed myself to doing it when I sent for the rifle. A sahib has got to act like a sahib; he has got to appear resolute, to know his own mind and do definite things. To come all that way, rifle in hand, with two thousand people marching at my heels, and then to trail feebly away, having done nothing—no, that was impossible. The crowd would laugh at me. And my whole life, every white man's life in the East, was one long struggle not to be laughed at.

But I did not want to shoot the elephant. I watched him beating his bunch of grass against his knees, with that preoccupied grandmotherly air that elephants have. It seemed to me that it would be murder to shoot him. At that age I was not squeamish about killing animals, but I had never shot an elephant and never wanted to. (Somehow it always seems worse to kill a large animal.) Besides, there was the beast's owner to be considered. Alive, the elephant was worth at least a hundred pounds; dead, he would only be worth the value of his tusks, five pounds, possibly. But I had got to act quickly; I turned to some experienced-looking Burmans who had been there when we arrived, and asked them how the elephant had been behaving. They all said the same thing; he took no notice of you if you left him alone, but he might charge if you went too close to him.

It was perfectly clear to me what I ought to do. I ought to walk up to within, say, twenty-five yards of the elephant and test his behaviour. If he charged, I could shoot; if he took no notice of me, it would be safe to leave him until the mahout came back. But also I knew that I was going to do no such thing. I was a poor shot with a rifle and the ground was soft mud into which one would sink at every step. If the elephant charged and I missed him, I should have about as much chance as a toad under a steamroller. But even then I was not thinking particularly of my own skin, only of the watchful yellow faces behind. For at that moment, with the crowd watching me, I was not afraid in the ordinary sense, as I would have been if I had been alone. A white man mustn't be frightened in front of 'natives'; and so, in general, he isn't frightened. The sole thought in my mind was that if anything went wrong those two thousand Burmans would see me pursued, caught, trampled on, and reduced to a grinning corpse like that Indian up the hill. And if that happened it was quite probable that some of them would laugh. That would never do. There was only one alternative. I shoved the cartridges into the magazine and lay down on the road to get a better aim.

GEORGE ORWELL

Questions

1 What are Burmans? What had these Burmans come out to see?

2 Why had the elephant only just become interesting?

3 Why had Orwell sent for a rifle?

4 What were Orwell's feelings about the crowd he found following him?

5 Why did he not want to shoot the elephant? What did he originally intend to do instead?

6 What did the crowd feel about George Orwell personally?

7 What made Orwell change his mind and decide to shoot?

8 What did Orwell most fear from the crowd?

9 What help did the 'experienced-looking Burmans' (l. 75) give?

10 What do you think are the meaning of (a) paddy fields (l. 3); (b) 'must' (l. 29); (c) mahout (l. 31); (d) sahib (l. 54)?

Implications

11 Would you say that Orwell displayed any courage in this situation?

12 Why do you think the Burmans tended to laugh at the British?

13 In your own words explain what Orwell says happens to the white man in authority. What does he mean by 'He wears a mask, and his face grows to fit it'?

14 Do you think these Burmans enjoyed any advantage from having British authorities present?

15 Why have so many countries that were ruled by Britain, such as Burma, wanted to be independent?

INTERNATIONAL RELATIONS

Exercises

16 Write a conclusion to this story.

17 Put yourself in a Burman's place and describe Orwell as he appeared to you at the time of the event.

18 Make a list of Orwell's reasons for not wanting to shoot the elephant, and a list of his reasons for doing so.

19 Write a letter to a pen-friend from Burma who has written to say that he belongs to a superior race. Try to point out the dangers of such an attitude.

Discussion and Writing

Photograph No. 11 (facing page 130)

Tibetans in England. Comment on their dress and how far English appearances have crept in?

Why do you think these people are living in England?

Is this a propaganda picture? How much does the background influence its mood? Is it in keeping with that of the Tibetans? What might it be seeking to demonstrate, and to whom?

Does the camera tell the truth?

Describe how you would hope to be received and treated if, with other members of your family, you arrived in an Asian country to seek political refuge?

12 Responsibilities

¶ *What do you think is the most difficult thing to explain to your parents?*

¶ *What do you think your parents find most difficult to explain to you?*

¶ *How can a father be of most help?*

Strike the Father Dead

[Jeremy Coleman, jazz pianist, has been beaten up defending a coloured friend in a race riot. While he lies in hospital, his father, who has not seen him for years, visits him.]

'The last time I was in hospital, Jeremy,' the old man went on—so he did know who he was talking to!—'was in 1917. It was a field hospital in France; near Arras I think, though I was a bit confused when I was taken there and I never quite gathered where it was. I wasn't there long; my wounds weren't serious and I only stayed a week or so before I was shipped back to England. I went to an officers' convalescent home near Dover.'

Still I kept silent. I just watched his face. Something damn near the bone was coming out, and I prayed he wouldn't stop.

'Does the name "Vimy Ridge" mean anything to you, Jeremy?' he asked suddenly.

'A big battle in the First World War,' I said, keeping my voice as neutral and matter-of-fact as possible. That was all it did mean, anyway. I couldn't have told you which side won at Vimy Ridge, or what stage of the war it happened in, or anything like that. But I'd seen the name in print somewhere, and it had stuck.

'Five-thirty p.m., April 9, 1917,' the old man said quietly, quite obviously thinking aloud but doing it, so to speak, in my direction. 'We attacked on a fifteen-mile front, from Croisilles to the Souchez river. That was the beginning of the battle. It lasted six days, on and off. But not for me. I was fortunate: for me it lasted just twenty minutes. In the twenty-first minute of the British advance, I was hit by shrapnel fragments in the chest and shoulders. My right arm became useless and I began to bleed heavily, so that within a few minutes I was unable to stand for loss of blood, though I retained consciousness all the time.'

Just like me, I thought. Well, well.

11

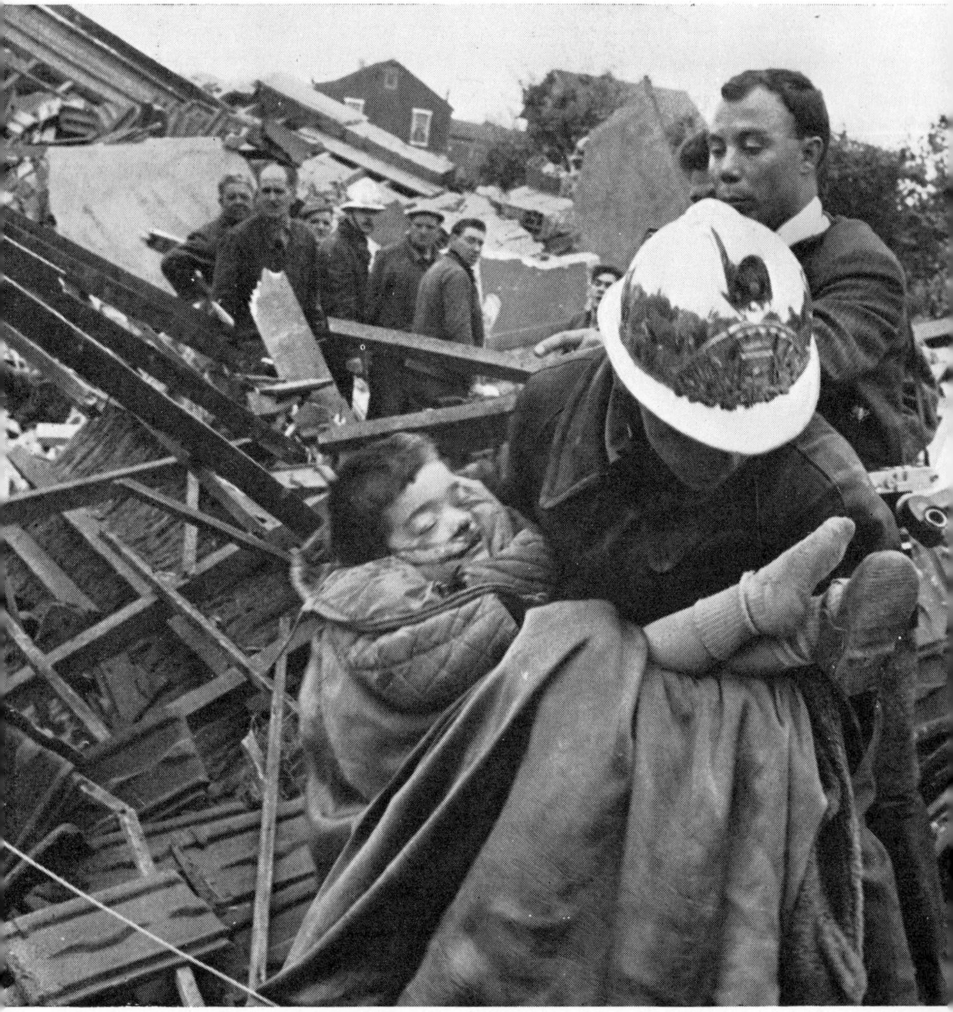

'I was taken back to the field dressing station by stretcher-bearers. Everyone was kind enough to accept without question that I could not stand by reason of the weakness resulting from loss of blood. To this day I could never quite answer that question in the silence of my own mind. It may have been fear that crumpled my knees and would not let me stand. It may have been the specific fear that if I did stand, if it did prove possible for me to remain on my feet, my duty as an officer would have been to lead my men forward.'

I lay as still as a mouse.

'At the time, I didn't think much about it. I don't think the question became real to me until the war had been over for ten years or more. At that time, I knew only that the attack on Vimy Ridge, which was not yet half an hour old, would go on without Second-Lieutenant Coleman. And the thought was sweet to me, Jeremy. I'd been through such a trough of fear and despair for weeks before the offensive. I fully expected to leave my bones in no-man's-land before the war was over; after about the end of 1916 we all expected it, and thousands of us were right. But in that spring of 1917 my courage had crumbled away. There seemed to be nothing to keep me going, no inner resources, no outward guidance. Time and again I used to wonder why I didn't take the revolver from my holster and simply blow my brains out, to be spared the agony of this waiting. And there were rumours of dreadful forms of death—we were in hourly expectation of gas attacks, for one thing. I had seen men who'd been gassed, and I couldn't sleep at night, even with the aid of whisky, for the memory of their faces.'

He was silent for a long time. I waited, knowing that an interruption now would be fatal.

'It was worse after Major Edwards was killed. He had been gone some months before Vimy Ridge. No death in all the war came to me with such tragic force. He was a brave man, Jeremy, who must have had such peace in his own soul that he could face death with a smile and a word of comfort on his lips for us younger men who found it almost too much to be borne. We all loved him. We never spoke of him after his death, but I had the feeling that all the junior officers—those who'd known him—lived hour by hour in his presence. He never left us, Jeremy, even after he was dead. It was only the spirit of Major Edwards that gave me the courage to move out of the trenches on April 9th. But even he couldn't make me stand on my feet again after the shrapnel hit me. And I'll tell you something, my boy, that I never thought I would tell any human soul.' His breath was coming fast and I wondered if I ought to call some sort of help, in case he had a seizure or something. But I thought it was more important to let him go on, and besides I wanted to hear what he had to tell me. 'As I lay there on the ground, in front of the strand of barbed wire I had been in the act of cutting, I asked Major Edwards to let me die. I actually heard my voice saying, "Major Edwards, let me go now: I can't face any more. I want to die and leave the war behind. Let me go now, Major Edwards, please!" I think I was still saying it as they took me back on the stretcher. I wanted so much to die, because I had ceased to be able to imagine any other way of escaping from the long-drawn-out brutality and hopelessness we were all trapped in—but even at that moment I felt I couldn't withdraw from the struggle without asking permission of Major Edwards. He was like a patron saint to us.'

'Or a father,' I said. I didn't really mean to, but the words came out.

'Yes, a father,' the old man went on. 'My own father was a fine man, but he had lived the life of a Victorian clergyman, and he could never have imagined anything like this. When I went home on leave, I used to be faced with blank incomprehension if I ever tried to convey to him an impression of what life was like for a serving soldier. He was full of high-sounding platitudes from the newspapers. I didn't blame him, because he had lived to middle age in a world that didn't contain anything of the kind. Mass slaughter, and mud, and trenches full of icy water, and lice, and corpses, were something he could never have imagined. The world he had lived in, and which he had served to the best of his ability, was an infinitely more peaceful place. Once the artillery started, once we came within sight of the wire, Major Edwards was the only father I had.'

I asked, 'Why didn't you ever talk to me about this before?'

'How could I, my boy, how could I? You were only seventeen when you left home, and one can't talk to a schoolboy about that kind of experience. And after that, we never had the opportunity.'

JOHN WAIN

Questions

1 What has prompted Jeremy's father to start talking about his wartime experience?

2 Why did Jeremy remain silent as much of the time as possible?

3 What did the name Vimy Ridge mean to Jeremy?

4 What evidence does the father give of his desperation during the spring of 1917?

5 When had Major Edwards been killed?

6 How did Major Edwards help Second-Lieutenant Coleman at the time of Vimy Ridge?

7 Why had Second-Lieutenant Coleman wanted to die? Why did he feel he had to ask permission of Major Edwards?

8 Why had Jeremy's father been unable to tell these things to his own father?

9 What are 'high-sounding platitudes' (l. 90)? What sort of platitudes do you think Second-Lieutenant Coleman's father used?

10 What two reasons does Jeremy's father give for never having spoken of this before?

Implications

11 What is a 'patron saint' (l. 82)? In what way is he like a father?

12 What does Jeremy's father mean by saying 'Major Edwards was the only father I had' (l. 97)?

13 What is there to indicate that Jeremy and his father had never talked in this way before?

14 'One can't talk to a schoolboy about that kind of experience' (l. 101). Are there certain things a father could not explain to his son? At what age would it be possible to understand the sort of horror that Jeremy's father is trying to explain?

15 Was it any easier for Jeremy and his father to understand each other than for Second-Lieutenant Coleman and his father? Can you give any reason for this?

Exercises

16 Imagine Jeremy going on to tell his father how he comes to be in hospital. Write the account as he might have spoken it.

17 Write a letter to yourself as you might be in twenty years' time advising how to treat a teenage son or daughter.

¶ *What is the most valuable possession you could ever hope to have?*

¶ *If your home were threatened with destruction and you had to leave it at once, what would you take with you?*

The Caucasian Chalk Circle

[In a revolt, Ironshirt troops murder the state Governor and wish to kill his family. The Governor's wife escapes with her wardrobe but forgets her baby, which is rescued by a servant girl, Grusha. When the Ironshirts track her down, Grusha tries to leave the baby with a farmer's wife—then thinks better of it.]

(Inside the farmhouse the stout Farmer's Wife is bending over the cradle when Grusha bursts in.)

GRUSHA: Quick, quick, hide it! The soldiers are coming. I left it on the doorstep, but it's not mine, it's from a rich family.

FARMER'S WIFE: Who's coming? What soldiers?

GRUSHA: I can't explain now. The soldiers that are looking for it.

FARMER'S WIFE: There's nothing to look for in my house. But I think we'd better have a few words together, you and me.

GRUSHA: Take the cloak off him, quick. It'll give us away.

FARMER'S WIFE: Take this, hide that! I give the orders in this house, my girl, so keep a civil tongue in your head. Why did you leave the child anyway? It's a sin that is.

GRUSHA *(looking outside)*: Here they are now, behind those trees. Oh, I shouldn't have run away, that only drew them on. What am I going to do?

FARMER'S WIFE *(also peeping out, shrinks back in terror)*: Mother of God, Troopers!

GRUSHA: They're after the child.

FARMER'S WIFE: But suppose they come in?

GRUSHA: You mustn't let them take him. Say he's yours.

FARMER'S WIFE: Yes.

GRUSHA: If you give him to them they'll stick their pikes through him.

FARMER'S WIFE: But what if they make me? I've got all the harvest money in the house.

GRUSHA: I tell you, if you give him to them, they'll murder him in front of your eyes. You've got to say he's yours.

FARMER'S WIFE: Yes, all right. But suppose they don't believe me?

GRUSHA: They will if you say it straight enough.
FARMER'S WIFE: They'll burn the roof down over our heads.
GRUSHA: That's why you must say he's yours. (*The Farmer's Wife nods.*) Don't keep nodding like that. And stop shaking or they'll see you're frightened.
FARMER'S WIFE: Yes.
GRUSHA: And stop saying Yes, it's getting on my nerves. (*Shaking her.*) Haven't you got a child of your own?
FARMER'S WIFE (*mumbling*): Away at war.
GRUSHA: Well, then, he's probably a trooper himself by now. How would you like him spearing little children? You'd soon give him a bit of your tongue. 'Stop waving that pike around in here, what sort of manners is that? And go and wash your neck before you speak to your mother.'
FARMER'S WIFE: That's right, he wouldn't dare.
GRUSHA: Then promise you'll say he's yours.
FARMER'S WIFE: Yes.

BERTHOLT BRECHT

Questions

1 How can we tell from what the Farmer's Wife says that she has kept out of trouble with the authorities?

2 What does Grusha most fear will identify the baby for the Ironshirts?

3 What are the first objections that the Farmer's Wife makes to Grusha and the baby being in her house?

4 What has led the Ironshirts to this house? Who is responsible for endangering it?

5 What will the Ironshirts do to the child if they find it?

6 What two things is the Farmer's Wife afraid of losing if the Ironshirts suspect her of causing trouble?

7 Grusha is afraid that the Farmer's Wife will betray the child. How might she do this?

8 Why does Grusha ask the Farmer's Wife if she has a child of her own?

9 When she hears that her son is a soldier, how does Grusha use this to rally the woman?

10 What has the Farmer's Wife undertaken to do by the time the Ironshirts arrive?

Implications

11   Both women are desperately anxious. For what? How do their anxieties differ?

12   Which of these two women has most to lose?

13   What right had Grusha to endanger a complete stranger's life and home?

14   At the end of the play it has to be decided who may keep the child—Grusha, or the mother who had deserted it and fled at the time of the revolt. How would you decide?

15   Could you guess where and when this incident might have taken place? How important is it to an understanding of the scene that this should be known?

Exercises

16   Make a list, in order of priority, of what you would take with you if your home was threatened with destruction and you had to leave it.

17   Write the scene that follows immediately after this when two Ironshirt soldiers enter. (It will help if you try to improvise the scene first, in groups of four.)

18   Write down, as briefly and plainly as possible, the statement that the Farmer's Wife might have given to the authorities about how she came to be involved in this affair.

¶ *Who is your neighbour?*

The most famous answer to this question, of course, was the following:

The Gospel of Luke

'A man was once on his way down from Jerusalem to Jericho. He fell into the hands of bandits who stripped off his clothes, beat him up, and left him half dead. It so happened that a priest was going down that road, and when he saw him, he passed by on the other side. A Levite also came on the scene and when he saw him he too passed by on the other side. But then a Samaritan traveller came

along to the place where the man was lying, and at the sight of him he was touched with pity. He went across to him and bandaged his wounds, pouring on oil and wine. Then he put him on his own
10 mule, brought him to an inn and did what he could for him. Next day he took out two silver coins and gave them to the inn-keeper with the words, "Look after him, will you? I will pay you back whatever more you spend, when I come through here on my return." Which of these three seems to you to have been a neighbour to the bandits' victim?'
'The man who gave him practical sympathy,' he replied.
'Then you go and give the same,' returned Jesus.

Translated by J. B. PHILLIPS

Questions

1 Was the Samaritan in any way obliged to help the victim?

2 What do you think the Samaritan should have done if he had arrived while the bandits were still beating up the traveller?

Exercises

1 Looking back over all the extracts used in this book, where do you find examples of 'practical sympathy'? In which extracts is 'practical sympathy' clearly lacking?

2 Write a short story about a modern 'Samaritan', bearing in mind that the people who heard the original story looked down their noses at Samaritans.

Discussion and Writing

Photograph No. 12 (facing page 131)
Why should a fireman risk his life to save anybody else's?
Who is responsible for the child in this picture?
Who is responsible for the fireman?

Write a poem entitled 'Who is responsible?'

Notes on Books and Authors

Many of the books mentioned in these Notes are available in paperback editions.

JOHN ARDEN has been one of the most successful young British dramatists. He won early recognition in a B.B.C. Drama competition and then wrote three plays for the Royal Court Theatre: *The Waters of Babylon*, *Live Like Pigs*, and *Serjeant Musgrave's Dance*. This last is available in a Methuen's paperback edition. It is about a group of three army deserters and their serjeant who pose as a recruiting party in a Northern mining town. Serjeant Musgrave is driven by an almost fanatical urge to expose the horror of war to the townsfolk. John Arden's most recent success has been *The Workhouse Donkey*, commissioned by Sir Laurence Olivier for the opening season of the Chichester Festival Theatre.

E. R. BRAITHWAITE is a teacher who comes from the West Indies. After serving in the R.A.F. he accepted a post in a school in the East End of London. *To Sir, With Love* is an account of the struggles he had to win the respect of his pupils. Mr Braithwaite has since been a Welfare Officer for the L.C.C.

BERTHOLT BRECHT has been one of the most influential dramatists of this century. He was born in Germany in 1898, wrote a large number of plays, poems and articles, fell foul of Hitler but returned after the war to direct the Berlin Theatre Ensemble and died in 1956. His best-known plays have been *Galileo Galilei*, *Mother Courage*, and *The Caucasian Chalk Circle*. The latter tells of a simple but courageous girl who rescues an aristocrat's baby in a revolution. She brings the child up as her own, only to find that the mother who abandoned him then claims him back. A judge is asked to decide who should keep the boy and he orders that the child be stood in a ring of chalk and the two women left to see who will pull him out first. He soon sees who has most care for the child's safety.

JOYCE CARY was born in Ireland, educated in England and as a young man served as an officer in the Nigerian Regiment. His first novel, *Aissa Saved*, was published in 1932, and from then on he produced a large number of stories and novels, including *Mister Johnson* and *The Horse's Mouth*. Several of his novels were written as trilogies, that is, sets of three independent novels, each one of which is told through the person of a different character from a group who appear in all three books. Joyce Cary died in 1957. In *Except the Lord*, a novel from one of his trilogies, Chester Nimmo, a future Prime Minister, recounts his childhood days and rise through the trade union movement to political power.

JOHN CHRISTOPHER was born in Lancashire, brought up there and later in Hampshire. After war service in the Royal Corps of Signals he worked in publishing and journalism. His first novel was *The Year of the Comet*, and he has also had a collection of short stories published under the title of *The Twenty-Second Century*. *The Death of Grass* was first published in 1956 and has been successfully adapted for radio. It is the story of what follows the death of all the grain plants in Asia and Europe as the result of a virus blight.

HAROLD ELVIN trained as an architect and then spent five years as Art Director and Floor Manager of the Elstree Film Studios. Since then he has worked as a ceramic artist, theatre-scenery painter, architect, farmhand, teacher of English abroad, and Company Secretary and Manager. He has bicycled through thirty countries. Harold Elvin is the author of seven books, including *A Cockney in Moscow*, a book about his experiences as Nightwatchman to the British Embassy and later as Assistant Films Attaché in Moscow during the war. He has won two literary awards, The Atlantic Award in Literature (Rockefeller Foundation Prize) for *A Cockney in Moscow*, and the Tom Gallon Trust award for a short story.

WILLIAM GOLDING served in the Royal Navy during the war, commanded a rocket ship and was in action against the *Bismarck*. After the war he became a schoolmaster and writer. In 1954 his *Lord of the Flies* caused an immediate sensation and has since been adapted for radio and film. In it a group of boys, evacuated by plane during an atomic war, crash on a tropical island and find themselves alone. Their attempts to organise themselves, their bitter quarrels and decline into savagery give a horrifying picture of how civilisation can easily break down. Other novels of William Golding include *The Inheritors, Pincher Martin, Free Fall*, and *The Spire*.

GRAHAM GREENE is one of the most widely known novelists of this century. He is a great traveller and most of his stories have a very strong sense of place. He started writing as a sub-editor on a newspaper; his first novel, *The Man Within*, was published in 1929. In 1938 he visited Mexico to report on the religious persecution there, and as a result wrote *The Power and the Glory*. It tells, in fiction form, the story of the last Catholic priest left in Mexico, his flight from the police, his loyalty to his calling and his final betrayal. Graham Greene has published over thirty volumes of novels, plays and stories.

SIR ARTHUR GRIMBLE was born in 1888. After leaving university he entered the Colonial Service and in 1913 was appointed as a cadet colonial officer in the Gilbert and Ellice Islands. He had a distinguished career and retired in 1948, perhaps little known outside the Colonial Service. It was when he gave a series of B.B.C. talks about his experiences in the Pacific that he became immensely popular as a story-teller. His broadcasts were often repeated and his book, *A Pattern of Islands*, containing much of the same material, was a best seller. It appeared in 1952 and is still in steady demand from young and old.

CLIFFORD HANLEY was born in Glasgow in 1922. He has worked as a journalist and script-writer for film and television. *The Taste of Too Much* is about a Glasgow boy, Peter Haddow, who lives in a corporation house and is trying to balance working for 'A' levels at school with his love for Jean Pynne.

JAMES KIRKUP was born in South Shields, the son of a carpenter. He went to grammar school there and to Durham University. His poetry became known to many people through broadcasting, which was an excellent medium for long narrative poems like 'The Descent into the Cave', an account of pot-holing in the Mendips, and 'A Correct Compassion', which described a heart operation he had witnessed. This last poem was written while he was resident poet at Leeds University for a year. *The Only Child* is a vivid recollection of his first ten years.

DAVID HERBERT LAWRENCE was born at Eastwood, the son of a Nottinghamshire miner. Both the extracts used in this volume spring straight from his boyhood memories. He won a scholarship when he was thirteen, but left school early to start work. Later he trained as a teacher at Nottingham University, taught for a while, but was soon living entirely from his writing. His first novel, *The White Peacock*, was published in 1911 and he continued to pour out stories, poetry, essays and novels until his death from tuberculosis in 1930.

LAURIE LEE was born and brought up in a Gloucestershire village. *Cider with Rosie*, which he dedicated 'To my brothers and sisters—

the half and the whole', describes his boyhood. Laurie Lee was first known as a poet, but achieved wide fame with the publication of *Cider with Rosie* in 1959. He has since bought back and lives in the cottage that he was brought up in and that he describes in *Cider with Rosie*.

CARSON MCCULLERS was born at Columbus, Georgia, U.S.A. in 1917. Her novel *The Heart is a Lonely Hunter* was published in 1940 and highly praised. Her most famous novel is *The Member of the Wedding*, which was published in 1946 and has since been adapted as both a play and a film. *The Ballad of the Sad Café*, published by Penguins, is a short novel about a curious trio in a small American town—a hard-hitting woman store-keeper, the little hunchback who steals her heart, and the husband who had left her after one day but returned later to settle accounts.

ARTHUR MILLER, another American author, was first known as a novelist, but is more widely recognised now as a dramatist. *All my Sons* won the American Critics' Circle Award in 1947 and the following year *Death of a Salesman* was acclaimed in America and England. Miller says he spent ten years thinking about *Death of a Salesman*, but wrote it in six weeks. The salesman is Willy Loman, a man who has lived on the American dream of prosperity while fighting all his life against debt and failure. Other plays include *The Crucible* and *View from the Bridge*. He also wrote the film script for *The Misfits*, which starred his wife, Marilyn Monroe.

LESLIE NORRIS was born in South Wales in 1921. His interests as a boy included playing club football and writing poetry. He is a teacher of English at a Teachers' Training College.

GEORGE ORWELL was born in India in 1903. After going to school at Eton and serving in the Burma Police, he rejected the ideas of upper-class leadership and imperialism, leading a life as near down and out as he could. He wrote and fought against fascism and dictatorship, was wounded in the Spanish Civil War and died in 1950. His best works are *Animal Farm* (1945) and *Nineteen-eighty-four* (1948).

J. B. PHILLIPS is an Anglican clergyman, scholar, journalist. His first translation of scriptures to be published was *Letters to Young Churches*, the letters of St Paul. When this appeared in 1947 its freshness and force in modern, often colloquial, English caused widespread public interest. Since then J. B. Phillips has gone on to translate the whole of the New Testament into English of our time.

NOTES ON BOOKS AND AUTHORS

ALEXANDER SOLZHENITSYN. Stalin's notorious prison camps were never openly admitted to by Russia until Khrushchev was firmly in power. Khrushchev's drive for greater personal freedom for Soviet citizens caused him to condemn Stalin's totalitarian methods, and for the first time others were allowed to join in the attack. One of the most significant pieces of evidence of this 'thaw' was the publication in Russia of Solzhenitsyn's *One Day in the Life of Ivan Denisovich*. Writing from his own bitter experience, Solzhenitsyn detailed the events of one day in a forced labour camp in mid-winter.

MURIEL SPARK was born and educated in Edinburgh. For some time she lived in Africa but returned during the war. She has written novels, plays, poetry and short stories including *The Ballad of Peckham Rye* and *The Bachelors*. 'The Black Madonna' is a short story in the collection of her stories published by Penguins as *The Go-Away Bird*.

JOHN STEINBECK is a Nobel Prizewinner and one of the best known of American novelists. *The Grapes of Wrath* was written in 1939 and told of a whole community's migration west from Oklahoma to California, driven from their overworked farm lands in search of work and food. During the war Steinbeck worked in England on the staff of the *Daily Express* and wrote *The Moon is Down*, a fictional account of one Norwegian town's occupation by Hitler's troops. Other books include *Of Mice and Men*, *The Pearl*, and *The Wayward Bus*.

GEORGE STURT took over his father's family business in 1884 when he was no longer young enough to learn the skills of wheel making as an apprentice would do. He did however know the work intimately and valued his master craftsmen highly. After giving up business he recorded what was by then a dying tradition in *Change in the Village*, 1912 and *The Wheelwright's Shop*, in 1923.

FLORA THOMPSON was born at Juniper Hill, North Oxfordshire, in 1877, the daughter of a village craftsman. She described village life as she knew it, from her own early days until the time she was assistant post-mistress of Candleford Green, in three books: *Lark Rise*, *Over to Candleford*, and *Candleford Green*. The first of these appeared in 1939, and later all three were printed in one volume as *Lark Rise to Candleford*. Flora Thompson died in 1947.

MARK TWAIN must have led a boyhood full of adventures like those of his own Tom Sawyer and Huck Finn. He was born in 1835 and his real name was Samuel Clemens. He became a boat-pilot on the Mississippi and when later he took to writing stories he adopted as a pen-name 'Mark Twain', the cry of the leadsman at the front of a steamer calling to the pilot that the water was deep enough for a passage. *The Adventures of Huckleberry Finn* is a longer but more rewarding book than *The Adventures of Tom Sawyer* from which it grew. Mark Twain died in 1910.

JOHN WAIN, novelist, poet, critic and broadcaster, first made his name with *Hurry on Down* in 1953. This story of a young man, with a degree he finds useless, wandering in search of a way of life, aroused great interest when it appeared. *Strike the Father Dead* is a later novel about the relationship between a young jazz pianist and his father, a university professor. John Wain was a university lecturer until 1955 when he resigned to give all his time to writing.

REX WARNER is a poet, critic and novelist who has won a name as one of the finest translators of classical literature. Perhaps his best-known translation in use in schools is *Men and Gods*, Greek stories taken from the Latin poet Ovid.

EVELYN WAUGH made his name between the wars as a writer of satirical novels, the best known of which are *Decline and Fall*, *Vile Bodies*, *A Handful of Dust*, and *Scoop*, a novel about journalists.

H. G. WELLS was born in 1866 at Bromley, Kent. His parents intended that he should become a draper, and much of the boredom and frustration of his apprenticeship is recorded in *Kipps* and *The History of Mr Polly*. He broke away from drapery to study and teach science and was soon writing articles and stories in large numbers. Though Wells went on to write on political and social themes, he is best known as the English father of science fiction, with *The Invisible Man*, *The War of the Worlds*, *The First Men on the Moon*, and many short stories. Wells died in 1946.

XENOPHON was a young Athenian Greek who in the fourth century B.C. joined an army of Greek mercenaries hired to fight in a Persian civil war. When they were in the heart of Persia, two thousand miles from home, the prince whom they were serving was killed in battle and the Greeks were quite cut off. To add to their troubles, the Greeks lost their own senior officers in an ambush. The army then chose Xenophon as its leader and he not only brought the ten thousand home, but wrote an account of the adventure afterwards.